Everyone Is Entitled to My Opinion

David Brinkley

Published by Random House Large Print
in association with Alfred A. Knopf, Inc.
New York

Library of Congress Cataloging-in-Publication Data

Brinkley, David.
Everyone Is Entitled to My Opinion / David Brinkley.
p.   cm.   ISBN 0-679-75905-0
1. United States—Civilization—1970–
2. United States—Social conditions—1980–
3. Large type books.   I. Title.
[E169.12.B697   1996]
973.92—dc20   96-11944   CIP

Random House Web Address:
http://www.randomhouse.com/

Printed in the United States of America
24689753

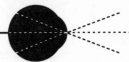

This Large Print Book carries the
Seal of Approval of N.A.V.H.

Dedicated to my perfectly splendid family: most
of all with the deepest love and respect
for my wife, Susan,
the wonderful woman who was always there
and always able to get it all together and make it work,
and with the greatest love and affection
for our children, Alexis, John, Joel and Alan;
my daughters-in-law, Evangeline, Sabra and Kate,
her daughter Maeve and our two grandchildren,
Katie and Elly

Acknowledgments

These small essays are chosen from among a fifteen-year collection of the odd, amusing and unusual in my closing minute or two on the ABC news program *This Week with David Brinkley.* We informally call them "homilies" for no very good reason. Simply, they are my comments at the end of the programs, broadcast in the hope of leaving our television audiences in a slightly better frame of mind than if we had left them with depressing thoughts of war, murder and drugs..

The Sunday program was in the first place the creation of Roone Arledge, president of ABC News. He pushed me—as well as Sam Donaldson, Cokie Roberts and George Will—along until we forced the dry and boring Sunday morning interview programs to straighten up. They did. For that we are indebted to Roone.

I am further indebted to Ashbel Green of Alfred A. Knopf for his help, support and encouragement with this and other books over the years. He was always there and always understanding. So was his brilliant assistant, Jennifer Bernstein, and mine, Jane Dickerson. To all of them, my thanks.

At dinner one night with several of my daughter Alexis's friends, all recent college graduates, I told them I was working on a book. They asked the title, as everyone does, but I had not found one I liked. I offered them a deal: a thousand dollars to whoever thought up an effective and appropriate title, whereupon Edwin Craig Wall III, one of the young people present, suggested the title now on the cover of this book. He wins the money and my thanks.

Introduction

Generations of us in journalism were taught the familiar, ritualized definition of news as it was handed down over the centuries, usually unquestioned and unexamined by those of us who came later. We accepted the word of the experts who stood ready at all times to offer opinions and stately analyses of newspapers' front pages and the content of news broadcasts.

What is the basis for this, for organizing and forcing into structured words and sentences the most mercurial phenomena in modern life and human behavior? It is difficult to find one.

Years ago I even welcomed the question put to me by an earnest young woman in some journalism class somewhere as she was struggling to put a name to the work she was doing when, suddenly, she said to me: "What about this? News is something worth knowing that you didn't know already."

Pretty good, I thought and still think. Her definition was interesting because it made its point simply and clearly in a few words. But still it left much to be argued about and to wonder about. And so it was a definition that did not define.

One of journalism's charms is that these questions can never be fully answered, even by the holiest and most revered eminence. They can only be discussed, picked at and argued about, preferably in the bar after the paper's printed and the news broadcast sent on its way.

The opinions offered here—mine—are the reason for this book. I did not set out years ago to collect cute little stories. In thirty years of broadcasting news and other stuff on NBC News with Chet Huntley and now at ABC News with the highly talented group of Sam Donaldson, Cokie Roberts and George Will, none of us on either network ever enjoyed the luxury of reporting on any single category of news—medicine, finance, foreign, sports. Many journalists prefer to specialize in, say, finance, because they then don't have to keep up with everything else. Finance is their beat. Everything else is somebody else's. In my own work I have, for better or worse, always dealt or tried to deal with everything that falls under the heading of news. Just news. No specialty, no emphasis on this or that or anything else. Just whatever came in. Anything. Maybe this is a legacy of learning my trade on a small newspaper with a staff of two or three and no more, with the result that we knew a little about everything and everything about nothing.

The Associated Press printer runs every day and all night. The result—an endless roll of paper carrying news and everything that can loosely be called news. The AP's clientele around the world is so vast it can send out almost anything and safely assume that somebody somewhere around the world will find it interesting and useful enough to print or broadcast.

My work for years has been to read, or at least to skim, this daily torrent of news and other stuff on paper. Tons of paper. Miles of paper. And since every news agency of any description is limited in space and time, selectivity is required. And since every newsperson has, or thinks he has, a vague notion, right or wrong, of what kind of people are in the audience, he puts out whatever news he thinks will appeal to all these people he has never seen. For these fifteen years I have worked for ABC News on a Sunday morning program called *This Week*. It is not a news program in the usual sense. It is interviews and talk. We spend most of the hour of airtime on what we think is the most interesting news story of the week, exploring it with interviews of those involved and with extended reports from the scene of the event.

In rummaging around every day through this tonnage of news material (news material, not necessarily news) and then discarding most of it, I find it useful to keep an eye out for the novel, the astounding, the amusing, the incredible. The man the police found living in a trailer with eighty animals, ranging from two turtles and thirteen dogs to three bears and other assorted wildlife, all left alone and seemingly happy in their own tiny and fiercely crowded zoo until the neighbors complained and called the police. They came, took the animals away and left the man there alone with his wife.

This was a small piece of news the AP slipped in on its wire, paying little attention because it did not fit into any professionally recognized category of "news." Neither did the discovery of a fifteen-year-old boy who ran away from home and took up residence in the bottom of an apartment building's elevator shaft—a place where nobody ever looks. He lived there with furnishings he had slipped in during the night and equipped himself with a folding cot, an electric hot plate, a television set and other amenities. He stayed there happily until the building's other tenants began to wonder why every night the elevator smelled of hot dogs cooking.

Oh, we keep up with elections, tax increases, foreign wars, major crimes grisly enough to be reported beyond the county line and the daily menu of minor horrors inflicted on us. All of this has to be gathered, evaluated and distributed to newspapers, magazines, radio and television, and it is all done with admirable efficiency. But beyond that, there are events that will never appear on the front page and will never be the lead story on a news program. They may be called the sauce, the spice, the flavoring to be mixed in with the wars, the medical discoveries and the economic upheavals that fill the front pages. But when they are there, the daily news report is a more accurate and often more interesting reflection of daily life in America and beyond.

Everyone Is Entitled to
My Opinion

I'd like to deal, if possible, with the cliché of the week. This week's cliché is that the Reagan honeymoon is over, and let us ask, "What does that mean?" if it means anything. It is a cliché because it is said sooner or later of every president. It was said wrongly of Franklin Roosevelt after a few months, and of every president since—except Jimmy Carter, who never had a honeymoon—and now Reagan. This week House Speaker Tip O'Neill made it official. He announced the end, as a saloonkeeper announces to the drunks at the bar that he is closing the door and the happy hour is over. The end of a president's so-called honeymoon is supposed to mean that he will no longer be able to persuade Congress to do anything unless it was already planning to do it anyway. But the truth is that after Roosevelt's honeymoon ended he presided over the establishment of Social Security, the regulation of the stock markets and World War II. The post-honeymoon Eisenhower sent the Army to integrate Little Rock's Central High School, and built the interstate highway system. The post-honeymoon Lyndon Johnson put in place most of the Great Society that we are still trying to pay for, built fences around the junk-yards and went into Vietnam. What the term "end of the honeymoon" really means is that there is an election year coming up, and Congress wants to position itself to vote with or against Reagan, as the politics dictate. So the term is not only a cliché, it is baloney.

Everyone Is Entitled to My Opinion

That was a short and very unhappy life for Saudi Arabia's peace plan. Pathetic, in a way. After fourteen years of rejecting every other peace plan, here at last was one that came from deep inside the Arab world. It was rough; it demanded that the Israelis give up almost everything but their shoes and socks, and Israel rejected it. Rough, yes, but it did at least state some terms on which the Arab states would let Israel live in peace for the first time. Outside the Middle East it got some support, in Western Europe and here in the United States, where it even drew a few cautiously kind words from President Reagan, and it did seem that it might be a basis for negotiation, or at least a starting place. But no. Nothing. The Arab leaders called a meeting—a three-day meeting—to discuss it in Fez, Morocco, but the atmosphere was so steamy with hostility the meeting ended in about three hours. Even the Arab states on the Saudi payroll rejected it. So all of this may suggest that much of the Arab world—Syria, Iraq, Libya—needs Israel as an enemy. Needs it. Without it, what would they say in their speeches to whip up the crowds? How could they get quoted in the world's press and interviewed on television? Without Israel, would the rest of the world ever again pay any attention to them, particularly those with no oil to sell? What would they find to do with themselves? What would Yasir Arafat do for excitement—or do for a living? Well, now that the Saudi peace plan is dead, we can see that it was never alive.

President Reagan is at Camp David setting pen to paper and deciding what to say to Congress and to the public in his State of the Union speech Tuesday night. Camp David is a poor place to work. The beauties of the woods, the mountains, the stone fireplaces with blazing hickory logs are more conducive to idleness and daydreaming than work. But he has to do it. There is a deficit of $100 billion ahead, lying there like a land mine. Cutting spending that fast is politically impossible. He took office promising to cut taxes and did. He cannot change his mind and raise them again a year later, but he also took office promising a balanced budget, not one $100 billion in the red. So now we are told, subject to change, that he will transfer more programs to the states, even though the states don't want them—can't pay for them, they say; can't even pay for those they already have. Well, Washington can't either, but the idea, beginning long before Reagan, is for Washington to dump the programs from its years of extravagance on the states and let them take the political heat for cutting them down, or the political heat for raising the taxes to pay for them. And the states have been a little extravagant themselves. In twenty years their payrolls have tripled. Writing a speech and finding the answers in a political situation like this is about equal to mud wrestling with alligators. So what'll he do? I don't know. We'll hear on Tuesday night.

I would like to say a word or two about the Philadelphia *Bulletin,* which died this week at the age of 135, and the Washington *Star,* which died last year at the age of 128. And several other newspapers are struggling to survive. When a newspaper expires, the death notices always give one reason for its demise—a change in American living patterns; that people going home at night don't read the newspaper so much because they look at television. Well, if that is true, and it probably is, nobody in television news takes any pleasure in it. On the contrary, since our whole lives are devoted to helping people find out what is happening, it saddens us to see a newspaper devoted to the same work lie down and never get up. Television is faster and more vivid, and it doesn't arrive wet on rainy mornings, but the papers can deliver a far greater volume of news than we can. How would all those columns of stock market figures play on television? Poorly. Television, newspapers and a hundred other interests compete for the public's time—the only thing everyone has in precisely the same quantity. That is about the only area of competition between them. But it is not a game, and it is sad if one wins at the expense of the other. No one regrets seeing newspapers die more than we do.

There is a lot of show business—posing, pos-
turing, pantomime—in this annual Washington
budget ritual, and it began long before President
Reagan. As popular light entertainment, however, it is lacking, because from the first act to the
last it takes about a year and a half—so long that
when the last act arrives nobody remembers
what happened in the first act. So there is a lack
of dramatic continuity. For example, in the six-
ties, when the numbers were smaller because Social Security was not then included in the
budget, Lyndon Johnson arranged to leak the
news that there was an epic struggle in progress
in the White House, a veritable *High Noon* starring Johnson in a white hat. We were told that he
was in the corral sweating and struggling like a
cowboy trying to rope a bull, trying to hold the
budget under $100 billion. High, exciting drama.
There were all these pressures to spend, we were
told, while he, the lonely cowboy battling in the
sun, choking on the dust, raising blisters on his
hands, was trying to hold on to the rope and
hold down spending. It was wonderful: Gary
Cooper could not have played it better. Then he
sent Congress a piece of paper saying the budget

was $98 billion. Actually, it was $137 billion. But by then who could remember the first act? Well, this week, with Mr. Reagan's budget going to Congress, we'll see this year's first act. The last act will be in the fall of 1983. What will we see then?

A new poll shows that a majority of people middle-aged and younger believe that when they're old enough to collect Social Security, they won't get it. Whether or not that is true, many people believe it is true and that the assurances they've been given were lies.

Of course, the tradition of governments lying to their people is an ancient one—ancient, hallowed, encrusted with its own traditions, rituals, orders, courtiers, keepers of the flame and experts who can sit down to a typewriter and write four pages of lies before breakfast. Some 2,352 years ago Plato wrote, in *The Republic,* that if anyone at all is to have the privilege of lying, it should be the leaders of government. It is a privilege they have freely exercised, down to modern times. For example, whatever happened to those Asian boys Lyndon Johnson said would do the fighting in Vietnam that American boys would not do? The balanced budgets we've been promised for years? Whatever happened to that 18 1/2-minute tape?

Well, are they lying now about Social Security? No. They can't lie about it because the figures are there and can't be hidden. It is running out of money. And the only solution is to put in more money or pay out less or both. And lies won't help. A little political courage will.

They don't want to do it, but they have to. To cheat people out of pensions they've spent their working lives paying for in good faith would be a swindle so massive no government could survive it.

A word about the continuing lamentations about Washington's bureaucrats. There is never a day without them. Reagan ran against them and won. So did Carter. The lament is always that they're overpaid and underworked, that whatever they do is not done for the public but for themselves, and so on. Well, this is not strictly an American lament. It flows, like air pollution, around the world. The world's worst bureaucracy, in my opinion, is the Soviet Union's, next the French, then the British and then the Spanish. They're all horrible. But it has remained for the Chinese this week to make a holy crusade or bloodless revolution out of what in other countries is only a running, keening complaint. This week Vice Chairman Deng Xiaoping pronounced his war against his bureaucrats to be a revolution, presumably bloodless, because, he said, they're ruining the country. Why? A Chinese government report says, "They love flattery, refuse criticism, are complacent and fuzzy-minded, have no interest in the masses, are covered with the dust of bureaucracy, arrogant, conservative, lazy, interested only in pleasure and privilege: servants of the people now ride on the backs of the people, tyrannically abusing their powers." Well, if after 3,000 years the Chinese have all those problems, what have we after 200?

The English language this week acquired an old phrase with a new meaning, courtesy of President Reagan. The term is "sob sister." In a speech this week he said those who complained that his budget cuts hurt the poor were sob sisters—those with vested interests in a permanent welfare class, vested interests in a government program that keeps people in a state of dependency. Well, for those of tender years, the term sob sister—in its old meaning—was a woman newspaper reporter who was only allowed to write stories about divorce and sick children and family tragedy, and this was intended to reduce the newspaper readers to sobbing into their breakfast oatmeal. The term was often used in the thirties in old movies about newspaper heroics, usually starring Lee Tracy, usually drunk. Of course, that was long before Betty Friedan and the ERA and NOW, and it is a term you certainly would not hear now from Lou Grant, the television newspaperman. One aspect of having a president a little older than average is that he remembers those ancient terms. But remembering them is one thing and using them is another. This one recalls an old-time sexual stereotype. It will annoy women. It confuses one public issue with another and gives his enemies another switchblade to turn on him. Perhaps his speech-writer was not old enough to know what it meant.

March 7, 1982

There was a pathetic little scene in the U.S. Senate this week. One senator was working crossword puzzles; others were reading the newspapers; and one was autographing pictures of himself to send to the voters back home, while Senator Harrison Williams of New Jersey held the floor for five hours pleading with the other senators not to expel him. He is a convicted felon facing three years in prison, caught as he was in the Abscam trap. He argued that he was a victim of entrapment, that the FBI enticed him and other members of Congress, set up concealed cameras, and offered bribes, which many took. Well, the FBI's methods may not be admirable, but it was not enticing the innocent and the naive but members of Congress, none of whom is on welfare, none of whom is on food stamps, and all of whom know there is crooked money around for those willing to take it. And they were invited to unlikely places around Washington and confronted with phony Arabs and others they did not know, including a loud-mouth con man. Even for members on the take, if all that didn't raise their suspicions, then they're too dumb to be in Congress. The record does show that Congress has not made a habit of expelling members for being dumb, but those both dumb and crooked have very little to offer in governing the United States.

Everyone Is Entitled to My Opinion

This week the Democrats adopted some new rules for their next presidential nominating convention in 1984. But as a survivor—and that is the word—of sixteen presidential nominating conventions, they should have asked me. I would have urged them first to enforce their ten-minute rule for speeches. Your average ten-minute convention speech runs twenty or thirty minutes. The way to enforce it is to put a trapdoor under the speakers' rostrum, and after ten minutes it flies open and the speaker drops through the floor onto a mattress. Democrats and Republicans should remember that at Gettysburg in 1863 there were two speakers, two orators—Edward Everett and Abraham Lincoln. Everett spoke for two hours, Lincoln for about three minutes. Lincoln's address is still remembered somewhere, but the Democrats seem not to have learned the lesson. Their new rules deal only with who gets into the convention—how many elected officials, women, minorities and so on. All very nice, but no rule on what happens once they're in. A twenty- or thirty-minute speech might be all right, if you only had to listen to one, but on any evening there may be ten. A country that can put a man on the moon certainly can build a trapdoor.

Everyone Is Entitled to My Opinion

The United Nations has published a report saying it is concerned about its image around the world, as well it should be. Its image now is that of an international body dominated by the Third World countries intent first on improving their own economic situations and, second, on using the U.N. to punish their enemies. Their current enemy is Israel. An atomic energy agency of the U.N. voted to kick Israel out for reasons having nothing to do with atomic energy. The next move will be to throw Israel out of the U.N.'s telecommunications union for reasons having nothing to do with telecommunications, and, ultimately, an attempt to throw Israel out of the U.N. itself. The immediate cause of all this is the murders in Beirut. But whatever blame may be laid on Israel, it does seem that to the Third World members in the U.N. only their enemies commit crimes. The following U.N. member countries, in peacetime, by government decree, have murdered far more people than were killed in Beirut: Iran, the Soviet Union, Argentina,

Liberia, the Central African Republic, Uganda and others. But there is no thought of kicking any of them out of the U.N. Why do you suppose that is?

A small and totally nonpolitical event this week that probably will not affect the course of human affairs. In New Haven, Connecticut, a fifteen-year-old boy ran away from home and, having no place to live, set up house in an apartment building at the bottom of the elevator shaft—a place where nobody ever looks. He brought in a bed, lights, stereo, a hot plate, books, magazines. He rigged the elevator telephone so he could call outside; he rigged the controls so he could park the elevator on higher floors to get himself more headroom; and he might have lived there forever. But the tenants riding the elevator wondered why they were always smelling hot dogs cooking. Nobody could figure it out. Finally, an elevator repairman found him and they moved him out—furniture, stereo, hot dogs and all. Well, a boy as ingenious as that might, when he is old enough, run for Congress and wind up answering questions on this program. I certainly hope so.

The session of Congress beginning tomorrow may not do much—a little bread and a few circuses—but it may well vote a 5-cent increase in the gasoline tax, the idea being to repair highways, bridges and so on, and to put some of the unemployed back to work. Practically everybody says it's a nice idea. But the Democrats want to spend the money where unemployment is highest; the Republicans want to spend the money where the repairs need to be made. And the two are not always in the same places. Another question: people out of work for months, with their unemployment compensation running out, need jobs now, but planning highway and bridge construction can take months or a year. Some outdoor work can be done only in good weather. More delays. And nobody knows how many of the unemployed know anything about building bridges, roads and tunnels. Restoring public facilities long neglected may cost a trillion dollars. The new gas tax would raise only a tiny fraction of that. So it is a classic Washington dilemma. There are people who need work; there is work to be done; but there is not enough money, this kind of work is slow in starting, and the people who need work may not be those who know how to do it. And, inevitably, it's another pork barrel—with members of Congress using their knees and elbows trying to get the money spent in their own districts. So it's another Washington program almost everybody says is a wonderful idea. It is, but not very.

Dr. Enrico Fermi, an Italian physicist working in a university laboratory in Rome in 1935, was the first to split the uranium atom. His work won him the Nobel Prize in physics, and Mussolini's Fascist government allowed him to fly to Sweden to accept the prize. He did, but he then exchanged his return ticket to Rome for a ticket to the United States, where, on December 2, 1942, he and a group of forty-two scientists working under an abandoned football grandstand at the University of Chicago produced the first chain reaction necessary to make an atomic bomb. Well, this past week, on December 2, the survivors of that group, now forty years older, came together at a reception in Chicago to recall, but not they said, to celebrate, that day. Said one of them, the atomic bomb is like a millstone around our necks. They were not there to celebrate what they did and what has been done with it since. A physics professor at the University of Chicago said, "We're not here to celebrate anything, except perhaps the intellectual power that made it possible." Another said, "The atmosphere was so different then. We were surrounded by a world at war, and to win the war anything you could do was justified." Well, many of those present forty years ago and this week, seeing what has happened since, want a worldwide nuclear freeze of some kind or a control of some kind, but don't really know how to get it. That's what they were saying in Chicago on the fortieth anniversary of a piece of history many people wish had never happened.

This week in Hartford the Connecticut Mutual Life Insurance Company found that in one of its departments its employees were spending 20 percent of their time on the telephone taking business calls. Tuesday is their biggest day in terms of paperwork because a lot of mail arrives on Monday, and so the company put out a new ruling: no phone calls will be accepted on Tuesdays. Anyone who does call gets a recorded message saying call back Wednesday.

On this same subject, the late Mrs. Alice Roosevelt Longworth, one of Washington's most admired women, would not accept a phone call until she had slept late, read the papers, dressed and had lunch—about one o'clock. She would not even talk to presidents until then. A Washington leader in the labor movement complained to me the other night that the phone would not let him get any work done. Well, I asked him, how many of these callers are offering to do something for you, as opposed to asking you to do something for them? He answered, "Zero." Still, people always answer because there is in the human heart always the hope that the next phone call will bring good news. Your son or daughter got a job, somebody left you money, or you've won the lottery. More likely it is somebody selling detergent or asking to borrow a screwdriver or offering free tango lessons. My one-man special commission on this telephone problem, a little simpler than Social Security, now publishes its official report. It says if you're busy, let it ring.

We might all hope that 1983 is a good year in all respects, 1983 standing alone, because it doesn't need any troubles of its own. It will inherit enough from 1982, and none of them will go away at midnight this Friday. The year 1983, for example, will inherit a recession spread around the world—12 million unemployed, the first soup kitchens we have seen in a generation. It will inherit a Washington establishment spending close to $200 billion it does not have; a Congress that would like to bail itself out by raising taxes but can't; a Social Security system that if not rescued will very soon run out of money; and various industries—automobiles, steel and so on—devastated by imports at least equal in quality but lower in price. And more. Our town here, Washington, regardless of who is in power, cannot fix all of this. But after a generation of promising to solve every social economic ailment, it has led people to expect Washington solutions, and so it will try a number of them. The good news is that the mathematics of probabilities shows that if they try hard enough, sooner or later, by accident or otherwise, somebody will do something right. It does seem that it's time, preferably in 1983, for the probabilities to go our way.

January 9, 1983

Perhaps the most startling piece of news this week was the announcement by the U.S. Post Office that it had made a profit for the first time in living memory—a rather large one. And so, maybe for once in our lives we can use up a roll of stamps before they raise the price again. But one reason they made money, they said, was there's been a big increase in third class mail, commonly called junk mail, which people say they don't want; it clutters up the mailbox, and so on. I would like to offer a small dissent and say that third class is the best kind of mail, because in third class you don't get bills; you don't get complaints from Internal Revenue that you haven't paid enough; you don't get letters telling you that somebody is sick or has been fired and so on. You never get bad news by third class. You only get good news—a chance to subscribe to *Time* magazine at half price, offers to sell you Lawrence Welk records, storm windows, tango lessons. And first-class mail you have to pay attention to. You have to answer it—you have to pay the bill, you have to pay the tax—

while third-class mail requires you to do nothing. If you don't want what they are selling, drop
it in the trash. I'll take third-class mail every
time.

Even with all of our problems, this past week could not have been all bad when we had, as we did, a candidate for president who promised that if elected, he would give every person in the United States—man, woman and child—$10,000 cash. His name is Lester Byerly, he's a housepainter in New Jersey, and he has filed the papers to run for president. It is worth noting that neither Walter Mondale nor John Glenn nor Gary Hart nor any of the more famous candidates has offered anything so attractive. He calls it "trickle-up" economics. Well, Lester, it's a nice idea; it's generous, and very democratic, since everyone gets the same amount—$10,000 for David Rockefeller and $10,000 for a baby one hour old and on welfare. My calculator cannot handle figures this big, but if my arithmetic is right, Lester's promise would cost $2 trillion 400 billion, give or take a few billion. Where does he plan to get all that money? Print it, he says. Just print it. It is hard to say what a dollar would be worth if they printed them like that, by the carload. Maybe a nickel. This may not be the world's best idea, but at least we know in clear, precise terms what Lester would do if elected.

What would Mondale and Hart and that bunch do? Who knows? So far they have not offered us so much as a quarter.

January 30, 1983

An early report on this year's technological progress. New automobiles on display now at the New York Auto Show talk a lot, and in three languages. That is, a lot of the new cars have electronic devices that imitate human speech and give the driver in words all kinds of messages, such as "Your headlights are still on," or "In another forty miles you will be out of gas." Chrysler has cars that will talk to you in three languages—English, Spanish and French. Ford has cars that not only talk but listen. You put the key in the switch and say, "Turn on the headlights," and it does. Or you say, "Open the trunk," and it does. Well, the Japanese, two or three models ago, had electronic voices saying, with a slight Japanese accent, "Please fasten your seat belt."

Well, now that this is the new gimmick in American cars, and in the imports, perhaps the level of automobile conversation might be expanded or elevated. Maybe they should say something slightly more interesting. They might, for example, say, "Please ask somebody else to drive. You are too drunk," or "Since you lit that cigar the air in this car is terrible. Please open a window," or "Attention, please, you're three weeks behind in your car payment." Now, that would be progress.

Here it is only the first week in February 1983, and we already have the first candidate announcing he is running for president in the election of November 1984, which is a year and nine months from now. Senator Alan Cranston of California was the first, and there'll be others. We count a minimum of seven in all, plus some fringe candidates, including Harold Stassen, I assume, since running for president is for him a hobby, just as collecting stamps or carving soap is for others. It is interesting, by the way, to contemplate that since he began running in 1948, he has been a candidate in more than 20 percent of our national elections since George Washington. In any case, there are four things this year that we can take for granted next year. One, the campaign for president now costs so much money that if it were a commercial enterprise it would be listed in *Fortune*'s 500. Two, even though the rate of inflation and the cost of living is down, the inflation in politicians' hopes and dreams of glory is still rising, by my estimate, at around 20 to 30 percent a year. Three, every Democratic candidate will attack Reaganomics unless, by some miracle, by next year Reaganomics becomes a success, in which case they will have to attack something else. And, four, whatever they attack, we can be confident no candidate in either party will say in clear, precise terms what he would do instead. For the political year of 1984, this is your first warning.

Muammar Qaddafi, the dictator in Libya in North Africa, has been quite busy. He has sent his oil money to support terrorists in Western Europe who like to set off bombs in crowded airports. Every day he demands the total destruction of Israel. He said Libyans living abroad must come home or be liquidated, and he has murdered a number of them in Italy, Greece, West Germany, Britain and the United States. He sent troops to support Idi Amin, the blood-thirsty thug who was committing wholesale murder in Uganda. When he ordered all private shops closed and the shopkeepers protested, he killed one hundred of them. He is said to be eager to acquire nuclear weapons. Last year the White House got reports he had sent a hit squad here to kill President Reagan. He harbors airplane hijackers and other killers and refuses to turn them over. He invaded Chad to his south and still occupies a part of it. He has threatened Tunisia to his west; he tried to invade the Sudan once and now is apparently trying to invade it again. And this week he said if the U.S. Navy comes near his coast he will turn it into a sea of blood and fire. Now, you've got to admit that's quite a busy record for a country 95 percent desert with a population of 3.5 million, two-thirds of whom are illiterate. Busy and nasty. We have often heard reports that Egypt would invade Libya and dispose of Qaddafi using American weapons. Those of us who think it would be a good idea wonder what they're waiting for.

The antitrust division of the Justice Department under a previous management spent several years pulling apart one of the few services left in this country that worked—the telephone company—and started us on our way toward using Japanese telephones along with Japanese everything else. Well, fresh from that great triumph of public service, the current head of the antitrust division, William Baxter, has another proposal somewhat less destructive, but a good deal sillier: when the chief executive of one business talks to the chief executive of another business, all their phone conversations should be recorded on tape. He is afraid that when they talk to each other they will talk about fixing prices in violation of the law, and so the tapes could then be used against them as evidence in court. Business people already know that if they agree to fix prices they can go to prison. Some already have. So if they really wanted to take the risk and do it anyway, and if they had to tape their phone calls, obviously they would not do it on a telephone. They would do it on a golf course or in a bar or somewhere they could be alone. And suppose they did tape all those phone calls. Who is going to listen to all those tapes? Another thousand bureaucrats sitting all day with tape machines and earphones? Wouldn't that be the world's most boring job? And the most unnecessary? Yes. In our continuing annals of bureaucracy, what great idea will the antitrust division offer us next?

The Constitution calls for electing a president every four years, but it does not say we have to spend the whole four years doing it. But that is about how it has worked out, and it has become a full-time industry that almost never stops. Walter Mondale has been running privately and publicly since election night, 1980. John Glenn's first handshaking visit to New Hampshire was in 1981. And there are others.

Beginning tomorrow, March 14, 1983, the Republican party more or less officially starts its 1984 campaign. It'll spend $100 million for television commercials in forty-five cities calling attention to the improvement in economic news and hoping for some political benefit. And the election is still more than a year and a half away. There seems to be no way to hold them back, either party. Well, here's an idea that might work: when the candidates first start making small noises about running for president, send them all up in a Goodyear blimp with some bottled water, Spam, Ritz crackers and clean shirts, and require them by law to stay at least 1,000 feet off the ground until one month before Election Day. Then they'll be allowed to come down. While they float around they could hang out of the blimp and shout down promises to anybody who will listen; they could float over baseball games and drop handbills. That would keep them safe, quiet and out of the way until October 1984. Then they could come down; we'd look them over and elect one of them. I've heard worse ideas.

This week the Democrats in control of the House Budget Committee met to vote on their policies concerning future taxing and spending. And they made it into a down-home, old-time 1950s-style Democratic fish fry on the levee. Voting for what they've always wanted—higher taxes on the higher incomes and more spending for government pay increases, social welfare and so on, and promises of more and bigger in the future. Well, they hadn't had a drink of that sweet fortified wine in about two years, not since Reagan came to town, so it's been a long dry spell for them and they loved every drop of it. The Republican minority on the committee was voted down on party-line votes one time after another. It was all very pleasing but for two inconvenient facts. One is that the government is already $200 billion in the red this year alone. The other is that the American people as taxpayers have begun in wholesale numbers to cheat, out of resentment of a tax system they think is unfair, too complicated and wasteful of their money. The so-called underground economy is growing rapidly—people working for cash only, reporting nothing, paying nothing.

Internal Revenue figures the loss this year will be more than $100 billion, and more next year. Presumably, then, if taxes are increased, the cheating will increase. So the Democrats had a wonderful time voting for more spending and more taxes, but their next problem will be to force people to pay them.

This week's news from Japan: the world's most eager exporter and most reluctant importer now says it'll make it a little easier for Americans and others to sell merchandise there. Seventeen laws that interfere with imports—Japanese imports—will be relaxed. The trouble now is that even an American product better than the Japanese equivalent—and there are a great many of them—cannot be sold there until they have inspected and certified it. One example: baseball bats. Now, how do they certify a baseball bat? I don't know. Do they ask a batter to hit a few pitches with it to see if he can hit doubles to centerfield? Well, if so, that would certify the batter more than it would certify the bat. Japanese businessmen always say the Americans can't sell much there because they don't bother to learn the culture and don't bother to learn the language, which is no doubt true. But to my own personal knowledge it is possible to make a first-class baseball bat, a Louisville Slugger, without knowing a single word of Japanese. So that complaint is nonsense and always was. The truth is they simply don't want to import anything but raw materials, which they then make into finished goods and sell back to us. Free trade is not possible when it is only one-way, and it is more than likely that with these policies of the past, wide-open Japanese access to one American market after another will not last much longer.

In Washington this week the Highway Traffic Safety Administration gave us a piece of distressing news. Fifty-eight people on separate occasions were driving their cars around, minding their own business, when suddenly and without warning their rear axles and rear wheels fell off—just fell off. And some of these cars were only two or three years old. The agency says the same problem and the same danger exist in several million cars. In recent weeks it has reported on others whose brakes tend to lock tight, power steering that fails without warning and so on. One line of cars has been recalled a dozen times. The Japanese have captured about a third of the American automobile market. Their cars cost a little less than ours, but not all that much, and they don't look any better, maybe even not as good. So why are they so successful? It must be because people believe them to be better built and more reliable. A layman who is not an automotive engineer might wonder, why is it that the American automobile industry, after eighty years of experience in building cars, finds it so difficult to keep the wheels on and to make the cars safe and dependable. Nobody expects a complex mechanical device to be perfect all the time, but this is ridiculous.

Most members of presidential Cabinets in both parties are men and women of terribly serious mien, often looking as if they're on the way to a wedding or a funeral or a prayer breakfast. You understand, the problems of the world are too grave for jokes. But every presidential Cabinet needs a clown, a member willing to make a perfect fool of himself to get people laughing, willing to behave like a jackass to give Washington something new to talk about. So if every Cabinet needs a clown, Mr. Reagan has got one. His name is James Watt, and he is the secretary of the interior. He is so good at it that Mr. Reagan must have got him out of Hollywood's central casting. He's got the easiest job in the Cabinet. The Interior Department does not start wars; it does not collect taxes; it does not send people to jail. Its duties include watching over flowers, fish, birds, trees, streams. Its National Park Service, in my opinion, is the best agency of the U.S. government. But many people think Watt does the job poorly, as when he ruled that the Beach Boys could not perform at the Washington Monument on the Fourth of July, because he thought they would attract a mob of crazy hippies with a lot of dope and crime, when in fact the Beach Boys would more likely attract the members of the Chamber of Commerce. This has now been explained to him in words of one syllable, and he seems finally to understand. Watt may not be our best secretary of the interior, but he certainly is our funniest.

A reporter once figured out in advance that a politician was going to announce something that day because he showed up wearing a blue shirt, meaning that he expected to appear on television. This goes back to the old days of black and white television; now any color will do, but for some reason the politicians still believe in the need for blue. So the Senate will become a sea of blue shirts if it decides to let cameras into its chamber. It has been arguing about it this week. Those against it—for example, Senator Russell Long of Louisiana—say if TV is allowed in the Senate, the members will begin to pose and posture and make long speeches, which is interesting when you recall that Senator Long has made a few speeches himself. His father, Huey Long, once set a record of sixteen hours, filling time by reading cookbooks. If television had been in the Senate then, it's probable that Huey would not have got on the air. Too long, too boring and no pauses for commercials. Well, now Russell says TV would reduce the Senate's dignity. Besides, he says, most senators' speeches are too long already. Another man corrected him. "You mean most other senators' speeches are too long already?" The Senate will decide this the way it decides so much else: will it help them get re-elected or hurt them? The answer is hard to figure. If a senator says something clever and pleasing, he could use the tape in his campaign commercials. If he says something notably stupid, his opponent could use it. And they are capable of both.

Switzerland is seen around the world to have a cold, clear eye for money. Its franc is backed 200 percent in gold; they have the world's only secret bank accounts, which even their own tax collectors can't look at. When movie star William Holden was making millions and moved to Switzerland to escape American taxes, the Swiss tax people went to him and said, "How much do you want to pay us?" and he said, "How much do you want?" They said, "$25,000 a year." He said, "That's too much; what about $15,000?" Well, they settled on $20,000. That's what he paid, proving again that the Swiss government understands money and the U.S. government does not. They see taxes simply as a way to raise cash. The U.S. sees it as a moral exercise. The Swiss occasionally offer a tax amnesty, saying if you will come clean this year, any cheating in the past will be forgiven, whereas in Washington this week a House committee held a hearing on a tax amnesty, and the deal would be that if you came in and settled up for every quarter you have not paid since the day you started work, you will not be prosecuted. Well, the difference is this: the Swiss say, "Come clean this year"; the U.S. says,

"Come clean, with interest, back to the first dollar you ever made"—which is one reason why the U.S. is always short of money, always in the red, and Switzerland never is.

At the age of nineteen, in a summer job, I was covering the recorder's court in Wilmington, North Carolina. Court opened at 10 a.m.; the spectators were mostly elderly idlers—retired carpenters and so on—who had nothing else to do, all wearing white shirts, straw hats, smoking nickel cigars, taking off the cellophane, tying it in knots, throwing it to the spittoons and always missing. Judge Winfield Smith took his place on the elevated bench, the clerk made his little singsong announcement, and then came the daily collection of petty thieves, drunks arrested for committing a nuisance on the sidewalk, somebody charged with hitting somebody with a brick. The arresting officer took the stand and said he had accosted this individual in front of J. C. Penney or someplace; then the defendant told his side. He'd have a lawyer if he had $25 for the fee. If he didn't, Judge Smith asked the questions. In about ten minutes the case was decided, often less. Guilty or not guilty. The not guilties walked out and went to work if they had jobs; the guilties were hauled away to serve maybe thirty days on the county farm growing cabbage. Usually it was all over by noon. The not guilties were out in time to go to work; the guilties were at the country farm in time for lunch. Well, I have heard a hundred reasons why, on perhaps a larger scale, the courts can't be run that way now. And I don't believe any of them.

A little more talk about money, this time about a financial transaction so ingenious that it deserves attention. In London a man set up the familiar barricades and flags and then opened a manhole in the street and climbed down into it with his tools to work on a telephone line, a routine occurrence. Two other men, calling themselves Mr. Sanders and Mr. White, went to a dealer in gold coins and bullion and bought $1,200,000 worth of gold, paying for it with a check drawn on London's National Westminster Bank. Of course, the dealer called the bank to see if the check was good, but the man down in the manhole had cut through a cable and rigged the phone line so the call wouldn't go to the bank; it came to him. Well, he answered and said, why, yes, of course this check is good, Sanders and White are among our best customers. They handed over the gold; Sanders and White disappeared. A London detective, admiring genius when he saw it, said, "This is a magnificent crime."

After a good deal of dodging and weaving, the Senate finally faced up to doing what it hates to do; skittishly, sheepishly, it voted to raise its pay to the same levels as the members of the House. And then it voted to put a limit after six months on how much senators may take in fees for making speeches, because it is considered sinful for a senator to take money for speaking. The theory—more or less—is if a business group, say, pays him for making a speech, it has bought him. But what about the members of the Senate who are already millionaires—Edward Kennedy, Howard Metzenbaum, John Heinz and all the others. There are lots of them. There is no limit on what they can collect in dividends, interest, rents, royalties, etc. Nothing was said about that. Is it more sinful to take money for a speech at a General Motors meeting than it is to take dividends from General Motors? So a Senate vote that seemed to be an exercise in piety and rectitude actually was hypocritical nonsense. If there is a public demand for members of Congress to take a vow of poverty, it is not loud enough to be heard.

After a lot of stomping and shouting and arm-waving in Congress, with about half of the members trying to cut the third installment of the tax cut, they failed and it took effect on this past Friday. In spite of all the oratory about enriching the taxpayers and draining the Treasury, the facts are quite simple. The average working person with two children will save about $2.40 a week. What on earth are we going to do with all that money? Well, it'll buy a pound and a half of hamburger, if you buy the cheapest. Three loaves of bread, a five-pack of beer—not a six-pack. Or, with all that money Congress wanted to keep from us, you can buy half of one ticket to the movies. So if two people pool their savings, one can go and see it and come out and tell you about it. Or, if that is not appealing, you can buy two Big Macs and one soft drink with two straws. Or you can buy a pound of baloney. Perhaps more satisfying than the baloney we've been hearing from Congress. They spent all those weeks arguing about this? Yes.

Some time ago there was a poll asking people which professions and occupations they admired the most and which the least. Physicians and clergymen came in first and second; used car salesmen and politicians came in last and next to last. Used car salesmen and politicians. For years we have known that people held politicians in low regard, and Congress and its members lowest of all. Well, this week there was a new survey, a respected one, by the Institute for Social Research at the University of Michigan. There is some news in it, but not much. It shows that people feel a little better about the government and the people in it, but their assessment is still mainly negative. One question they were asked: "Do you think government wastes a lot of the money we pay in taxes?" Three years ago 78 percent said yes. Now it's better. Only 66 percent, or two-thirds. Another question: "Do you think government can be trusted to do the right thing most of the time?" Last time only 25 percent said yes; now it's way up to 33. Obviously the Washington establishment has so little support that if these were votes rather than poll figures, it would be voted out of office and sent home. And while this shows Washington is doing a little better, it still isn't fooling most of the people any of the time.

Everyone Is Entitled to My Opinion

Four scattered items in the news added up to more than the sum of their parts. First, the automobile industry reported higher sales and higher profits. Second, the automobile workers' unions, seeing those profits, demanded and got higher wages from Chrysler; and Ford and General Motors will come next. Third, some increases in car prices were announced. And, fourth, the Japanese automobile industry said when the limit on its exports to the U.S. expires next month, it does not want to renew it.

Well, what does all this add up to? To a suggestion that Detroit should concentrate, first, on building its cars better, and instead of dividing these new profits with union members, already well paid, on giving some thought to their customers, not by raising prices but by cutting them. If so, they'd sell more cars, put more of the union's people back to work, make money and put pressure on the Japanese all at the same time. In the industry, talk of price-cutting after ten years of raising them induces profuse sweating and trembling hands, but it makes sense, and it's time for it.

There was a press dinner here in Washington earlier this year. Among the guests was Interior Secretary James Watt; the menu was roast duck. After dinner, Mark Russell, the comedian, took the rostrum and said, "I want to announce that Secretary Watt personally wrung the necks of all the ducks served here this evening." Everybody laughed, including Watt. But this week the laughter has again been replaced by groans and demands for Watt's resignation. And he has sent out still another letter of apology. He probably ought to have these printed up in quantity as a form letter, since he uses them so often. As everyone has heard, he said in a speech that a new committee in his department was, as he put it, politically well put together because it was composed of "a black, a woman, two Jews and a cripple." You've got to admit, Watt does have a way with words, a way of choosing them carefully and choosing them wrong. Time after time, insult after insult. The only reason he is still here is that Mr. Reagan hates to fire people. Several Republican senators say they want him out, as he is an embarrassment and will be a political liability in the coming election year. One senator

did defend him, saying he should stay on because he understands the West. Well, no doubt.
But he has to survive in the East if he does.

From the annals of bureaucracy. Until a few years ago the federal government's fiscal year ended on June 30, but somehow Congress never managed to get all the appropriations bills voted out by then, so they changed it to September 30, giving themselves three more months. But now, in the year ending this past Friday night, they still didn't get it all done. Of the thirteen big appropriations bills, only six are finished. Parkinson's law, of course: work expands to fill whatever time is available for it. And so, what used to be called June spending is now September spending. If a government agency has any money left at the end of the fiscal year, it has to give it back to the Treasury. But they will do anything to avoid that. Anything. And so, in the last week of the fiscal year there is a wild spree of spending. If you have anything to sell, anything at all, bring it to Washington that week and they'll buy it, because they're desperate to get rid of the money. Several years ago the Pentagon spent some of its leftover money on punch cards for computers, buying a 460-year supply. They, incidentally, are now obsolete. And this past Friday, in one day, the Pentagon spent $425 million for various goods and services, perhaps including some of those famous $800 screwdrivers, because at Friday midnight it would have had to give the money back. So the debt rises, as it has for generations, and we have not yet paid for World War II.

The following is labyrinthian, Byzantine, complex and confused as only Washington can manage it. James Watt is much admired in the West; he's seen as a secretary of the interior who will take their side against a federal government often regarded there as an occupying power. James Watt is among the Republican party's most successful fund-raisers. Everybody in Washington and politics admires anybody who can raise money. They ask, "How can you get elected without it? Am I going to hitchhike to my next speaking date?" But despite all of his charms, Watt can put both feet in his mouth and chew gum at the same time. So he's become a Republican embarrassment and there's a resolution in the Senate asking that he be fired. But the Republicans don't want to have to vote on it. They've stalled and delayed, but they can't stall much longer. They don't want to vote against Watt and antagonize all those in the West who love him, including those who give the money. And they don't want to vote for him and antagonize those who feel Watt has insulted them. The only way to avoid this embarrassment is for him to resign, and so far he won't. That's Washington for you, and it's all ours.

It's pleasing to say a word about a recent crisis that doesn't involve any bombing or loss of life and cannot be traced to Moscow. And it's not urgent, it's 100 or 200 years away. The two reports we've had are on the so-called greenhouse effect, on how the burning of oil and coal releases carbon dioxide into the atmosphere, where it works like a greenhouse. It lets the sun's heat reach the earth and then holds the heat in. It means, they say, the earth will grow warmer. New York City will have a climate somewhat like Daytona Beach, Florida, which I guess is good. The heat will melt the polar ice caps and all that water will raise the level of the oceans, and so some low-lying land, including some here in Washington, will be underwater. Well, when this happens, people in boats won't notice it, but vacationers in beachfront hotels might find it wise to move up to the second floor. Unlike our ordinary crises, in this case we'll have plenty of time to think about it. Time for the liberals to blame it all on big business, time for the conservatives to blame it all on big government, plenty of time for government commissions to study the problem and issue reports. Now, that's my kind of crisis.

In the dispute with the Pentagon about the press, printed and broadcast, being barred from Grenada, the American people generally sided with the Pentagon, because they seem not to like the press much anyway, saying it's too left-wing, unfair, biased, inclined to push bad news and conceal the good and so on. So this week it has been interesting to see the political leaders in two states who love the press: Iowa and New Hampshire. Each is fighting with the Democratic National Committee; each is insisting that its presidential voting in February and March be ahead of the other states. Why? Because if they weren't, the press wouldn't pay much attention to them. I would not be so crude as to suggest they like the newspapers and the networks flooding in, spending money, filling up the hotels and the restaurants. I can't believe that is a factor. But the publicity certainly is. If Iowa's caucus and New Hampshire's primary got no attention outside the states, they wouldn't care about who was first. But they do care. There's a real fight about it. The candidates, when asked, as they have been, why they expend so much energy in two small states, why they go at all, have been known to answer, "We go because you, the press, go there." Because flattering public notice is to a politician what Tender Vittles is to a cat. The two states want to be first because they'll get more attention in the press. The candidates want to be there because they'll get more attention in the press. It's nice to feel wanted in at least two states, if only for a week.

We've had a curious little spat here in Washington this week at the White House. The Reagan folks, naturally, are pleased to see the economy improving—inflation low, unemployment falling, the stock market rising. All very nice, and good reason for the White House to be pleased. But then there is Martin Feldstein, the president's economic adviser. He keeps saying yes, but. The economy is doing well, he says, but there is a $200 billion deficit and high interest rates. Well, the White House crowd sees him as it would a relative who comes in for Thanksgiving dinner and says, "Yes, the dinner is fine, but the soup's cold." And so publicly they have all but told Feldstein to shut up or get out. Not because he's wrong. He's not. But because they want to accentuate the positive and eliminate the negative. They want to talk about the good economic news and ignore the bad—and who would not? Even though, when you go to the bank's loan window, it's hard to ignore the fact that they want 12, 13, 14 percent plus points.

Well, I have a suggestion for Feldstein. Hereafter, if they don't fire him first, he should say this: "Yes, the economy is good, and big deficits and high interest are good for you. Spending money we don't have is the American way. And paying 14 percent plus points forces you to work hard and builds character." The White House would just love it.

A football game is only a football game, with some very heavy players kicking and falling and catching and pushing each other around—a demolition derby without wheels. Except when the teams are the Dallas Cowboys and the Washington Redskins. Then, given the two best teams in football and their famous rivalry, it becomes an event of epic proportions before an audience of screaming Romans, including some wearing funny hats. Well, at least at today's game in Dallas, at Texas Stadium, which is something to contemplate. If you don't have a ticket, the classified ads offer them for sale at $300 each. Of course, you don't need tickets if you own what is called a circle suite. That's a private, enclosed box, heated, cooled and carpeted, including private bathrooms, kitchens, bars, big soft chairs in which to watch the game, and television for instant replays. One of these boxes recently sold for $1 million, a box 16 by 16 feet. That works out to a cost per square foot of $3,906.25. For about $100 a square foot you can build a first-class house. So it must be the most expensive real estate in the world. Of course, if you build a house you can't look out the front window and watch the Cowboys play the Redskins, and in Texas that's got to be worth a few dollars.

Everyone Is Entitled to My Opinion

Life in Washington this week. Edwin Meese of the White House had a good time on Friday. He came out with a pile of plastic trash bags filled with pamphlets printed by the U.S. government and given free to anyone who wants them: 1,800 of them, he said, and all of them were being killed off, eliminated, saving the government $85 million a year, the cost of printing them and paying the people who write them. One pamphlet is called *Controlling Bedbugs*. So far as I know, they are the only living creature having no Washington lobby to protect them, no office on K Street with lawyers, WATS lines, electric typewriters, thick carpets and grants from the Ford Foundation. But there is Ralph Nader. He said this would deny useful information to the poor, who are more likely to have bedbugs than those who live in Beverly Hills mansions, where the Reaganites came from. But there are other pamphlets: *How to Control Avalanches, How to Buy a Christmas Tree, How to Install Solar Heating in a Milking Barn*—no doubt useful to somebody, but in the quaint folkways of Washington this must be understood: Ed Meese got a chance to make a little show of saving money; Ralph

Nader got a chance to protest. In due time the bureaucrats will again be printing all of these pamphlets and more. And the $85 million? Nobody will ever see it.

Those large white mounds lying on desks all over Washington are piles of paper, recommendations for reducing the no doubt famous $200 billion deficit. They're from business groups, think tanks, university economics departments and Wall Street thinkers, and these mounds of paper have now reached a height of 2 feet 4 inches and rising. Those from right-wing sources say the answer is to cut the spending. Those from the left want to raise taxes on the rich. Wonderful exercises in ideology put in the form of charts, computer notes, footnotes, columns of figures. Right-wing charts competing with left-wing charts, and all of them offered with great assurance. One or another of them may actually have the right answer, just as one of the Wall Street investment people may have the right answer if only we could figure out which one it is. One element missing in all of them is this: this is an election year, and members of Congress are intent first, second and third on being reelected and are unwilling to vote for anything that will antagonize the public. The American people may not believe that reelecting a member of Congress is the most important business in the world, but he does. It's a fact of life in Washington, but I don't see it in any of these charts, footnotes or graphs.

A little history. In 1974 a bunch of the boys in the antitrust division of the Justice Department were sitting around, so to speak, passing the time of day, wondering what to do, and along came the brilliant idea to file an antitrust suit against the telephone company. They went to court demanding it be broken up, saying it was a monopoly in violation of the law. It was not. It was one of the few services left in American life that worked. This made no difference to them because they were intent on making a big score. After ten years in court, a billion dollars in lawyers' fees later, they now have their way. The phone company has been torn apart for a month and a half now, and already there are complaints from business and other users of declining service and rising costs. For home users the phone bill is a confused tangle of little slips. The charges go up; the service goes down. So who has benefited from all of this? Nobody I can see but the lawyers. My opinion is that those in the antitrust division should be locked in their offices, their phones cut off, food and water passed under the door. Then maybe they would leave us alone.

Lest it all become too serious and we forget the country will go on, whoever wins, the Democratic party loves to write rules. And in trying to be fair to all, it has written rules so complex, those it is trying to be fair to can't understand them. For example, for their convention in San Francisco they want delegates with all groups equally represented, on a tight mathematical basis. The "allocation factor," they call it. Well, fine. Here I am indebted to the *Wall Street Journal* for these computations, since a paper like that must know more about math than I do. So, Alabama. Alabama's allocation figure comes down to the number of .01572475. I think that means a one-millionth, five-hundred-seventy-two thousandth, four-hundred-seventh-fifth of a delegate. Well, where can they find delegates that small? An Alabama baby one hour old is bigger than that. As I say, nobody understands these rules. I certainly don't. But I do know if they can find delegates that size they can hold their national convention not in an auditorium but in a cigar box.

Years ago, after a few modest little scandals, President Harry Truman was asked if Washington officials shouldn't sign a code of ethics. He said no, that the Ten Commandments and the Sermon on the Mount were all the code of ethics anybody needed. So he signed nothing and never needed to.

But still, to this day, the Washington establishment has an occasional fit of morality and feels a need to put it all on paper and sign it. It must be because we have so many lawyers who tend to think nothing can be believed until it is on paper and signed.

So, presumably, if you wish to show your wife you do love her, the right way is to put it on paper and sign it, have it notarized and hand it to her. Not flowers and little notes, but a notarized document with stamps and seals on it.

In the spirit, the national chairmen of the Republican and Democratic parties gathered in some solemnity on Friday and signed a paper: a political code of ethics. The paper says their campaigns will not resort to personal vilification, character defamation or appeals to prejudice. Appeals to prejudice? Is it not true that congressional districts having a majority of people of one ethnic or racial or religious background tend to elect people having the same background? Is that prejudice for or prejudice against? If so, which one is sinful? This week's new code of ethics does not deal with this and none of them ever will.

So Harry Truman was right again.

Now there's a little lull in the political campaign and the candidates have time to consider the fact that their television commercials, which we've seen many times, have become a little boresome. And it's time for some new ones.

The old ones tried to frighten us, like the famous red telephone ringing, as if a war had started, while an announcer, paid union rates, was saying we needed a sure, tested, steady hand to answer that phone. Well, anybody can answer a phone. The question is, what does he do after he answers it, and that question was not answered.

Then there's the one with the picture of a burning fuse, like those on firecrackers. And an announcer says, "Remember Vietnam? Will we ever learn?" Learn what? That it was two other Democrats, Kennedy and Johnson, who got us into Vietnam? We already knew that.

How about a new announcer, one with a voice like warm maple syrup pouring out of a pitcher, who says something like this: "This candidate is the kind of man you would buy a used car from, one you would like to have living next door to you, who, if you were sick, would bring over a lemon pie, who promises if elected to keep the White House clean and not spill anything on the rugs. If he borrows money, he will pay the interest, if the banks insist. And if he gives people government jobs, it will be for all the usual, familiar, shabby, tawdry political reasons, not because they lent him money." Now, commercials like that we could believe.

This past week there were meetings among the big mules of the Democratic party—the national chairman, the former Democratic chairman, the candidates. And they were trying, they said, to settle the party's disagreements now, to avoid messy fights at their convention in San Francisco. Avoid messy fights? The Democrats? What kind of convention would they have without messy fights about who gets nominated; what the platform says; who gets to speak on television, mill in the aisles, ignore the speakers, wear funny hats, eat, drink, smoke? If they don't do all of that, how will they spend their time? Listening to organ music and reading the collected speeches of Walter Mondale?

I have a word of advice to the party leaders: turn back from this before it is too late. Stick to the party's long habit of having messy fights about how to soak the rich and how much to give to the poor, how many new bureaucracies to set up, how many new and unenforceable laws can be put on the books, how to spend the money, what sins and crimes they can find to blame on the Republicans. Messy fights, all of them, and all entertaining. Without them people

might tune in to television coverage of their convention and find it so orderly and peaceful they
will think they're looking at the Republicans.

"This production was brought to you by Tip O'Neill, producer and director"—the doings of the House of Representatives as shown on cable television. But the cameras are controlled by the House leadership, which means the Speaker, Tip O'Neill of Massachusetts, not by the television networks. Because O'Neill didn't want the cameras aiming around the chamber and showing the members working crossword puzzles, yawning or even falling asleep, he said the cameras had to show the member who was speaking and nothing else. Well, okay. Now the politics. Recently, late in the day, the Republicans have been accusing the Democrats of various sins and crimes, and O'Neill was irritated. So he sent new orders to the TV cameras: during these Republican speeches, pan around the chamber to show that nobody is listening, that in fact most of the members have left the room. They did, showing Republicans talking to an empty chamber. The Republicans were furious. They said it was a cheap political trick. Cheap or not, why did they care? Their speeches were intended for the audiences at home, not those present in the House chamber. If O'Neill really wanted to pull a political trick, cheap or otherwise, he'd have put in a laugh track, and when the Republicans make a point, bring up the laughter and the guffaws. Or he could drown them out with commercials and say he was helping reduce the deficit. All of us in Washington have seen worse.

From the annals of military bureaucracy. There's a disease the medical profession may not know about. It's another acquired immunity syndrome, an immunity to all reason and common sense acquired by those in government spending money that is not theirs. The prime symptom is an utter indifference to what anything costs, because as they see it, it's really nobody's money. For example, the socket wrench worth $1.49 the U.S. Navy bought for $466. So this past week Congress tried to grapple with this new set of outrages in Pentagon purchasing. Representative Jack Brooks of Texas is walking around with an Allen wrench, which sells in hardware stores for 45 cents, pinned on his lapel. The Pentagon buys them for $9,000 each. A diode, a tiny electronic part worth 4 cents, somebody in the Pentagon bought for $112. It gets worse. Those little plastic feet that stick on the bottom of the legs of metal chairs. They sell for 17 cents. The Pentagon buys them for $1,118 each. There are, of course, the usual expressions of outrage. What is not mentioned is that this kind of thing has come up year after year for at least twenty years. Has anyone ever been prosecuted for cheating the government this way? No. Is it surprising that more and more taxpayers are reluctant to finance this kind of insanity? No.

This past week Congress passed a fairly piddling tax bill so the members going home for the elections could say they did something about our world-famous deficit. They messed around with the taxes on whiskey, cigarettes and a little something on tax shelters—the easy ones. It may not do much for the deficit, but it will help to make the tax code even more incomprehensible. But next year, after the elections, they will have to do something serious. And there are at least 100 ideas on what they ought to do. Well, here is mine, the 101st. And admittedly it is dangerously radical. It is this: write a tax law simply to raise money, period. Don't use the tax code to manipulate people's lives, to encourage this or discourage that, to promote one social purpose or another. All of that can be done, if it has to be done, some other way. Just write the law simply and straightforwardly to raise money to pay for the government. That's all. Beyond that, leave people alone to do with their money as they see fit. It is theirs, isn't it?

A few words about military preparedness in years past. In the summer of 1940, in the pre–World War II U.S. Army, mainly composed of unwilling draftees, the 30th Infantry Division was sent on training maneuvers in the woods of Tennessee. War games during the day, sleeping on the ground in the woods in bedrolls at night. There were about 30,000 men there, but it soon appeared the men were outnumbered by the rattlesnakes. Since these were war games, they had rifles but no ammunition. The snakes were everywhere. Nobody could sleep for fear of having one crawl into his blanket. I was the supply sergeant in the 120th Infantry, and they came asking me for ammunition to shoot the snakes. I had none. I went to the commanding officer. He said, "Brinkley, you get these men shooting rifles all over the woods at night, they'll kill each other." And I said, "Yes, sir. But what about the snakes?" And he said, "Listen. The U.S. Army doesn't have enough ammunition to fight a war. It doesn't have enough ammunition even to kill these snakes." So we killed them with shovels.

Later, when a real war started, the Army was still unprepared and the Republicans put out a report blaming President Roosevelt and the Democrats.

Washington, we all know, is the land of the experts—those who, with great confidence, tell us what is going to happen. Those proven right will remind us of it and perhaps try to sell us a newsletter, while those proven wrong remain silent and hope we'll all forget. Mostly, perhaps, we do forget. But now the authors of a new book called *The Experts Speak* have gone back through the records and with vicious pleasure have recorded some experts' predictions from the past. Adolph Hitler's nephew in the thirties: "My uncle is a peaceful man." Lord Kelvin, the great British physicist in the nineteenth century: "Radio has no future." The *New York Times* correspondent in Moscow in 1920: "The Bolshevik government will not last six months." Abraham Lincoln, in 1860: "The South has too much sense and too good temper to break up this nation." The head of the U.S. Patent Office, in 1899: "Everything that can be invented has been invented." Jimmy Carter, in 1977: "Because of the greatness of the Shah, Iran is an island of stability in the Middle East." And my favorite, John B. Sedgwick, a Union Army general in the Civil War, seeing the Confederate Army open fire on his troops at the Battle of Spotsylvania, said he was not worried because "they could not hit an elephant at this dist . . ."

Since we'll all be up to our ears in politics, like it or not, for the next several months, and since we have just survived—if that is the word—two political conventions, here is a brief and obviously quite biased guide on how to tell a Republican from a Democrat. A Democratic congressman, Andrew Jacobs of Indiana, put this into the *Congressional Record*. If anyone knows a similar guide to the Democrats, I'd like to see it. This one says, "If a Republican catches a fish, he has it mounted and hung on the wall. If a Democrat catches a fish, he eats it. Republicans wear hats and clean their paintbrushes. Democrats do neither. Democrats give their old clothes to the poor. Republicans wear theirs." And, finally, the one I liked the best: "Democrats name their children for people in politics, sports, entertainment. Republicans name their children for whichever grandparent has the most money."

Parkinson's famous law is that work expands to fill whatever time is available for it—an hour's work takes an hour if that's all the time there is. If there are four hours it will take four hours. Well, this week we have seen with extreme clarity Parkinson's law at work in the U.S. Congress.

First, a little history. Until the late thirties, Congress routinely adjourned for the year in late April or May or early June and went home—partly to escape the heat of Washington summers. Then, in 1938, they air-conditioned the U.S. Capitol and since then we have had what amounts to a permanent, year-round Congress.

Well, with so much time available, everything takes even longer. The government's fiscal year used to end on June 30, meaning Congress had six months to get all the money appropriated, but they just couldn't do it. So they moved the date to September 30. This week we saw they could not do in nine months what they couldn't do in six months. The more time available, the longer it takes. Senator Daniel Patrick Moynihan of New York asked, "What has happened to the Congress? Why can it not do its work?" Nobody answered, even though it was clear they can't get anything done because they have too much time. Here's the solution. By law, turn off the Capitol's air-conditioning on Memorial Day, May 30. The fear of Washington's summer—damp heat, shirts sticking to their back—will force them to do their work and get out of town.

For those who may not have noticed, this is the fifteenth anniversary of one of the great philosophical insights of modern times, the Peter principle. It was in 1969 that Laurence J. Peter wrote his book propounding the great truth that in business, government, education and the military, people are routinely promoted to the highest levels of their incompetence. For example, if you're a good salesman, they promote you to sales manager. If you're good at that, they make you a vice president. If you're worthless at being a vice president, they don't promote you anymore and leave you in the job you have proved you cannot do. That explains, of course, why nothing works anymore—the Peter principle. Well, now Peter is out with a new treatment of his great work, showing that his principle has been in operation for years. He recalls that in the War of 1812 an American general named William Henry Winder led his troops into battle against the British in Canada. He had the British outnumbered four to one, but he managed to lose the battle and to get himself captured. The British quickly realized that a general so incompetent would do them more good on the other side, so they handed him back. Here the Peter principle functioned perfectly. Winder was put in command of defending Washington, D.C., against British attack—still the same William Henry Winder. The British moved in on Washington, set fire to the White House and other public buildings and moved on, and Winder didn't notice anything until he smelled the smoke.

December 2, 1984

Washington's financial distress has brought out some particularly bad ideas on how to raise more money, and perhaps the worst can be found in several bills now in Congress proposing a national lottery similar to the state lotteries. Why is it such a bad idea? Every week or two we read that somebody somewhere has won a million dollars in a state lottery. But has he? Usually they pay him $50,000 a year for twenty years. In simple arithmetic, that does add up to a million dollars, but if they gave him the million all at once, at current interest rates he could collect $100,000 a year forever and still have the million. So in truth they don't pay him a million. They don't even pay him the interest on a million. Plus, when the federal and state tax collectors get through with him, they will have more of his winnings than he does. And the average state lottery pays out only about 40 percent of what it takes in. Las Vegas slot machines do better than that. So did the lotteries the Mafia used to run. If these state lotteries were under the jurisdiction of the Securities and Exchange Com-

mission, they might well be accused of mis-
leading advertising, if not fraud. To the four
congressmen pushing this idea the message is,
try again.

Everyone Is Entitled to My Opinion

One of the annual bores always appearing around this time of year is a list drawn up by newspaper and television editors of what they think were the ten biggest news stories of the previous year. Well, now here I am indebted to the Baltimore *Sun* for another idea—the ten most boring news stories of 1984. And in my opinion the *Sun* is right on all counts. Here are the ten:

1. Congress Fails to Enact Stop-Gap Spending Bill
2. Arms Talks Clouded by Uncertainty
3. Troubled Talks on Trade and Tariffs in Geneva
4. Panel to Weigh Democratic Delegate Selection Rules
5. Burger Complains of the Supreme Court's Workload
6. International Monetary Fund Mulls the Latin Debt Crisis
7. No-Fault Bill Wins Committee Approval
8. Critics Hit Campaign Spending

Everyone Is Entitled to My Opinion

I see in a letter from a member of Congress that the U.S. Air Force, by using competitive bidding in buying aircraft engines, has saved $5 billion. Well, fine. I figure that comes to $62 per taxpayer. So where is the money? Will they send each of us $62 or, in the case of joint returns, $124? Or will they send the money back to the Treasury with a nice little note saying, "Thanks, folks, but here's $5 billion we don't need"? Certainly not. They won't do either. What will they do with the $5 billion? They will spend it on something else. Over the years I have seen dozens of bureaucracies, military and civilian, announce with great pride that through efficient management and so on they have saved millions and billions. But nobody I know has ever seen a quarter of it.

The moral is this: the bureaucrats must stop saving money; the country cannot afford it.

Washington this weekend is talking not about the budget but about John Riggins. He is a football star with the Washington Redskins, and in this town the Redskins can do no wrong, except to lose a game. The Washington Press Club had a big dinner called "A Salute to Congress," with the whole business. A big hotel ballroom, black tie, silk dresses, a sea of round tables; Sam Donaldson, the master of ceremonies. Sam had some good jokes, but it was pretty much uphill from there. Heavy food, heavy air, smoke, heat, small talk. John Riggins was there and he'd had maybe a half a glass of wine or so. He got up from the table, lay down on the carpet and fell asleep. The waiters serving the tables just stepped over him, nobody said anything—after all, what was there to say? Nothing much, except that Riggins had got through a Washington function the way a lot of people would like to get through Washington functions—by falling asleep and waking up when it's over.

This week the U.S. Congress was terrorized to see piles of mail coming in from ordinary people—not lobbyists or organized groups but ordinary people complaining about something Congress had done. All the mail says the same thing. A new tax rule voted by Congress makes no sense, it's utterly silly and far more trouble than it's worth. The law says, for example, that a plumber who uses a truck in his work and deducts it as a business expense has to keep a diary of everywhere the truck goes for business purposes, fixing a leaky faucet, unstopping a sink, how many miles there, how many miles back and so on every day. It also applies to farmers with their pickup trucks, traveling salesmen with cars and all kinds of service people using cars and trucks. In one year this certainly would generate at least enough useless paper to fill an airplane hangar, and the man-hours spent filling out all these forms would cost more than the taxes raised. The public reaction is so furious that Congress probably will change the rule or drop it entirely, and then they can contemplate why they passed such a silly law in the first place.

This weekend most of the Democrats in the House of Representatives are in the Greenbriar Hotel in the mountains of West Virginia for a little group therapy on how to recover from their defeat last fall. Interestingly, one of the therapists they invited to come down and offer counsel was Lee Iacocca, chairman of Chrysler. The Democrats' thinking was that if he could turn around the Chrysler Corporation, maybe he'd have some ideas on how to turn around the Democratic party. Well, what he might have told them was that before he took over, Chrysler got into trouble because its cars were too big and too expensive to operate. So is the U.S. government. Iacocca trimmed them down, reduced their weight and size and improved their efficiency so the customers got more miles per dollar. The government might do the same. Chrysler had some big fat cars that looked like painted bathtubs upside down with wheels on them. Iacocca got rid of them. Washington has a lot of agencies and programs just as fat, heavy, clumsy and obsolete. Do they need Iacocca to tell them what should be done with them?

This is not a prediction and certainly not an expression of any real expectation, but more like a fleeting springtime fantasy. But suppose for a moment that the United States and the Soviet Union did, as is now discussed, settle all their differences. What would we do? Washington is full, for example, of think tanks, people specializing in global strategies and the geopolitics of war and peace. If peace broke out, what would the think tanks think about? What would General Dynamics do for a living? Of its $8 billion profit last year, $7.5 billion came from the Pentagon. Would it turn to making toy fighter planes and cap pistols for our kids to play with? Well, perhaps, but our kids can't pay Pentagon prices. And, not least, what would Congress do? It would face the terrifying task of finding ways to spend all the money it used to spend on defense. Could Congress face up to this arduous task? Yes. In finding ways to spend money it has never failed us.

Two small items from this week's news. The U.S. Air Force bought two pairs of pliers from the Boeing aircraft company. Boeing's price was $2,548 each. The Air Force objected and argued the price down to $748. At the corner hardware store, pliers are $7, $8 or $9.

Second, American negotiators are in Japan trying to persuade the Japanese to buy some of their telephones and communications equipment in the United States, where, after all, the telephone was invented. Since the U.S. Justice Department has torn apart the American system, and presumably is happy now that it has us using Japanese telephones, it might see if the Japanese selling phones here might agree to have some American phones sold there. But they are resisting, as usual. So here is a possible solution: we buy Japanese telephones, and the Japanese buy their pliers from Boeing. At Boeing's prices, we should come out about even.

We never see unanimous votes in Congress unless they're voting on mothers, apple pies or flags, but we did see a unanimous vote this week, and it was about none of the above. It was about trade, or the lack of it, with Japan. The Senate voted 92 to 0 to demand that Japan, if it wants to sell all that stuff here, open its markets and buy something from us. This was after Japan announced it would ship another half million cars to the U.S. in the next year, while the trade negotiators in Tokyo were trying to make some deals with them, and failed. In 1984 they sold to the U.S. $37 billion more in merchandise than they bought.

What are they, a small country, doing with all that money? I'm glad you asked. A lot of it—billions—they're sending back here to the United States, and with it they're buying U.S. government bonds. So we send the money over there, it comes back here and goes into bonds paying 12 percent interest. At 12 percent interest, compounded money doubles in six years. So we buy a Japanese car, we pay for it; in six years, with interest payments, we pay for it again. In less than twelve years we will have paid for it three times.

We thought it was impossible, but now we see that the Japanese have invented a perpetual-motion money machine designed to run forever, or at least as long as the American money holds up.

As we have heard, there is anger at Japan for flooding us with consumer products while refusing to buy anything much. As the head of a large American business said to me, "They are picking us like a chicken." Well, no doubt. But a little history is instructive. The transistor was invented in 1948 at the Bell Telephone Labs. What did we do with it? Because it was tiny, we used it in hearing aids and very little else. The Japanese went to Bell Labs and bought the right to use the transistor, for which they paid $25,000. By now they have got that back a billion times or more. There is not a single transistor radio made in the United States. Not one. The tape recorder— German technology brought back here by the U.S. Army. The Japanese came across an army pamphlet about the tape recorder and thought, "Well, maybe people might want these at home to play music." Now there isn't a single consumer tape recorder made in the United States. Videotape recording—invented in the U.S. All of those we buy are Japanese. Automobiles—invented in Europe; the mass production invented by Henry Ford. Virtually everything we buy from Japan was invented or developed here.

Everything they are selling us we could have made ourselves. But we didn't. Questions about Japanese trade policies, yes. But we also need questions about American business management, unions and U.S. government policies. Why aren't we selling transistor radios to the Japanese?

Senator Jake Garn of Utah spent several days flying around the earth as a passenger in the space shuttle *Discovery,* and he came back down saying it was so great he would rather be an astronaut than a senator—which, if he is serious, probably could be arranged. But in Washington, a cynical and uncharitable city, some would recommend that maybe the whole Congress, all 535 of them, should be put in orbit for a while. It might be a little crowded in a spacecraft designed for about ten people, but anyone who didn't like crowds would never have gone into politics in the first place. And you have to admit, it is engaging to imagine all of them drifting up to the ceiling at zero gravity, floating loosely in the air, making speeches about a new tax bill while upside down. More important, it's the only place on earth or anywhere near it where the lobbyists and special interests could not get to them to argue for more and bigger loopholes. It's the only place, for example, where it is possible to write a decent tax bill. As they say, if we can put a man on the moon, we could put Congress in orbit.

In the 1930s the North Carolina legislature had a bill before it saying the theory of evolution could not be taught in the state schools. One member who opposed it defeated it by saying, "This bill's only purpose is to relieve the monkeys of their responsibility for the human race." Well, he was a small-town lawyer named Sam Ervin. Later he came to Washington, to the Senate, carrying the King James Version of the Bible and the Constitution, having memorized both, and he quoted both of them frequently. He presided over the Watergate hearing that led to Richard Nixon's resignation, and then he retired and went back to his law practice in Morganton, North Carolina, where this week he died. And a very large crowd turned out to honor him. A few years ago I went down to do a little interview with him in his law office, which was in his house. It had high ceilings, very high, maybe 18 feet, and Ervin's law library shelves went all the way up to the ceiling. I said, "Senator, what would you do with a law case that requires you to climb up to get books on the top shelf?" He said, "I wouldn't take the case."

Some time ago General Motors announced it would build a new plant to produce a new car called the Saturn. This week GM said it was flooded with requests from more than a thousand cities and towns asking to have the new plant. I would like to add another name to the thousand and suggest they put the plant here in Washington. Not only could they build cars here as well as anywhere else, but General Motors would also be performing a public service. It would allow Washington to see for once what real work is—that is, real work as opposed to paper shuffling. This city is filled with officials with large offices and mahogany desks, bureaucrats, lawyers, lobbyists, people worrying about snail darters, think tanks that for a price will do studies and write reports telling you what you already know. So I think it would be healthy for Washington and the country if all these people could get a look at somebody doing real physical work, hammering, drilling, painting fenders and so on, to help them understand that while paper may have a purpose, you can't ride it. And, of course, to assemble cars you need screwdrivers. Here in Washington we already have them. We bought them for $800 each.

When George McGovern ran for president in 1972, he introduced into the American political vocabulary the term "the three-martini lunch." He was saying business people could take tax deductions for a three-martini lunch, but a working person couldn't deduct his baloney sandwich. Well, McGovern lost, but his phrase survived. It's a nice populist term to be used in speeches in Congress, on the campaign stump, in pious editorials, left-wing assaults on business, funny newspaper cartoons and so on. It's used all the time. Jimmy Carter used to say that he didn't care if they drank three martinis, he only cared about who paid for them. Well, now Mr. Reagan's new tax plan limits deductions for food and drink, including martinis. I have never seen anyone drink three martinis at lunch, but I see from the mail that across the country critics of the Washington establishment wonder if they do what they do because they're all drunk. Well, no. They write all those complicated rules and regulations cold sober. If they'd had three martinis, they'd be even worse.

They're having elections today in Mexico to choose seven state governors, members of their Congress and others, and for about a week before today's vote, the opposition party has charged the government party with fraud, loading the voting lists with *fantasmas,* or ghost voters—names of nonexistent people, they say, names copied off tombstones or simply made up. The government denies it, of course, and says it's a computer mix-up. The only reason for going into this is that it's an excuse to tell an old story about Texas voting frauds, just across the border, and a story Lyndon Johnson used to love to tell. He said that before a Texas election a group of politicians carrying flashlights went into a graveyard at night to copy the names off the tombstones to put them on the registration rolls and to have them vote fraudulently. Well, they came across one stone, covered with moss that had been there a long time. The name was hard to read, so they skipped it and went on to the next one. Their leader said, "No, no, no. Go back and get that name. He has as much right to vote as anybody in this cemetery."

This summer we've had the worst series of airplane accidents and loss of life in memory, one after another. Many people have died in airplane accidents and fires, even on the ground, because they couldn't get out of the plane fast enough. The Federal Aviation Administration requires an airliner to have enough emergency exit doors to allow all passengers to get out in ninety seconds. This week we were told there had been a test of a Boeing 757, and a planeload of people got out in 82.9 seconds, just in time to meet the government's safety standards. But they were nearly all Boeing employees. All of them were youngish and reasonably agile. They had rehearsed ahead of time. There was no fire, no smoke, no poisonous gas or burning seat covers, no older folks unable to move fast, no babies having to be carried, nobody lingering, as people will, trying to rescue their belongings, no panic, no fear, and—not always true on airplanes— they were all sober. Even so, in these ideal circumstances, they barely got out in time to meet the government safety standards. This is supposed to make us all feel a little easier about airplane travel. Somehow it doesn't.

The *Congressional Record* is the daily printed report of the proceedings of the House and the Senate—speeches, arguments, votes and so on—and the rules allow a member of Congress to have a speech printed in the *Record* even though he has never actually delivered it. In the printed *Record* coming out the next day, it appears that he has made a rousing speech full of rhetorical flourishes, dramatic and poetic phrases, when in fact he has not said a word; he's merely handed in a written speech and had it printed as if he had delivered it. Well, three members of Congress and a few others, in a very unwise move, went to court and sued to have this kind of deception stopped. It corrupts the historical record, they said. This week a federal court wisely turned them down. I say wisely because what would happen if they had won their lawsuit? Every member of Congress would have to stand up and make these speeches, some of them an hour long and more. And somebody, even if only the clerks, would have to listen to them. For once justice has triumphed.

Another chapter from the annals of bureaucracy. A professor of political science at a university in Illinois writes me to say he was notified by the Social Security Administration that its records showed he was dead. He wrote back and said he was not. No response. He wrote again. No response. He wrote them and asked where and when he died and where he was buried, because he'd like to put flowers on his own grave. The information was denied. The professor then wrote to his congressman, Sidney Yates of Illinois. Yates called Social Security and they said they would reexamine the case. They did, and said they found their original determination to be correct and that he was dead. But it said he could ask for a hearing to contest this finding and present his side of the case.

After all the publicity, Social Security said it had been a computer mistake. That, of course, is the all-purpose excuse these days, not just at Social Security but at the banks, department stores and credit card companies. But this was a little different. On the Social Security computer your name and number and so on are in its memory, and when the time comes there is a key to press to inform the computer that you have died. But the computer has no key to bring anyone back to life. Social Security never saw any need for it since this hardly ever happens. I think they kept insisting the professor is dead because it's easier than figuring out how to correct the computer.

November 3, 1985

There are times when this city is difficult to understand. Two examples.

Last Sunday morning the government's passenger railroad, Amtrak, observed the end of daylight saving time, turning the clock back an hour, by stopping all of its trains with the passengers aboard at 2 A.M. wherever they happened to be and letting them just sit there for an hour waiting for the clock to catch up with them, they said. Otherwise, all their trains, they complained, would have arrived an hour early. Not an hour early in real time, but an hour early by the changed clock. So what's wrong with that? They obviously have no rule against arriving late. They do it all the time. So what's wrong with arriving early?

Another example, the so-called spaghetti war. We, the U.S., have raised our import duty on pastas—spaghetti and so on—imported from Italy. But the Italians buy their wheat from the United States, take it over there, make it into spaghetti, put it in little boxes, print pretty pictures on it, ship it here and sell it to us. We sell them wheat, they sell us spaghetti. It sounds like a perfect deal to me, and I don't know why we have to start a war about it.

With the election of a new Congress less than a year away, the Democrats are looking around for issues that will win seats for them in '86, they hope. So the party has just finished a very large poll of voter attitudes across the state, and across the country. They found the results surprising, but they probably shouldn't have. For example, they learned that the voters are sick and tired of hearing politicians' speeches about fairness because they have come to believe that fairness is a code word for one more expensive giveaway program, and that fairness means the middle class will pay for another program from which it, the middle class, derives no benefit, that all the benefits will go to others. It has always been an article of faith in this country that the American people will accept almost everything if they believe it to be fair. But after a generation or two of hearing the word used rather loosely and of seeing the debts and bills pile up, they seem to feel now that in public life, government life, fairness has come to mean something else. And so the Democratic party's new poll shows that when people are asked about fairness it seems their reflex is to grip their wallets and say, "Fairness, yes, but what's it going to cost me?"

Last summer a Japanese politician responded to American complaints about our huge trade deficit with Japan—the fact that they sell us a lot but won't buy anything. His response was that there was nothing in the United States any Japanese would want to buy.

Now, interestingly enough, he's been appointed Japan's minister of international trade and his job is to increase trade both ways. Even though his view is that we have nothing to sell them.

He's wrong, of course. He just didn't look far enough.

What about the new McDonald's hamburger with lettuce and tomato? In a box that keeps the hamburger hot and the lettuce and tomato cold? Nobody in Japan can match that breakthrough.

And what about the new Coke? Who else in the world would have the imagination—and courage—to mess around with the world's most popular soft drink and change the taste?

Or the electric clock that does not strike a gong on the hour but makes the sound of a dog barking?

And how about Hamburger Helper, which costs more than the hamburger?

There's plenty to buy here. The Japanese don't know what they're missing.

Ferdinand Marcos may not be the worst national leader ever forced out of office. There are many contenders for that honor. But he certainly must have been the richest.

He arrived in Hawaii with piles of cash, jewelry and all kinds of valuables, and left behind in Manila papers he didn't have time to pack, showing ownership of real estate in huge quantities. Members of Congress estimate that his assets were worth more than a billion dollars, and that his wife's were worth at least as much, or more.

There is not much doubt that a lot of this is money from American taxpayers, sent to the Philippines in the form of aid, and that nobody was aided except the Marcoses and their cronies.

In the future, it may be difficult to persuade dictators to leave, as in this case, if they know that all their money will be taken away from them. Look at Jean-Claude Duvalier, living it up in France in a luxury hotel with a whole crowd of his friends, having lobsters for breakfast in bed. How much other American aid money sent to Third World countries is stolen before it ever reaches the people it's supposed to help? A lot.

In case the record is not already complete, we learn today that Ferdinand Marcos not only cheated the Philippine government out of billions, hiding it in Switzerland and other places, he even cheated on his golf scores. M. J. Gonzalez writes a golf column for a Manila newspaper. He used to play eighteen holes with Marcos now and then. In his column, quoted in the Washington *Post*, he tells how Marcos did it. On the golf course, Marcos was always surrounded by a huge group of bodyguards. They would spread themselvesout along the fairway, presumably to keep intruders away from the president. Then Marcos drove off the tee. And after a shot that looked to everyone else as if it had been sliced into the woods, the players walked down there and found that, by some miracle, Marcos's ball was not in the woods but out in the middle of the fairway and much closer to the green than anyone thought it was. Not only that, if Marcos was behind, he had his caddy, who kept the scorecard, shave points off his score. And, finally, about the money. Gonzalez says Marcos always liked to bet on the games. Before he became President, if he lost he would pay his debt. After he became president, if he lost he refused to pay. Just one thing here is not clear: if his bodyguards kept moving his ball out to the fairway and closer to the green, and if his caddy was shaving his score, how could he ever lose?

The political news from west of the Pecos, from El Paso, Texas, and yesterday's primaries. There were five interesting candidates for various offices. Candidates 1 and 2 were just out of jail. Number 3 was in a psychiatric ward. Number 4 ran his campaign out of a saloon. And candidate number 5 was dead. Candidate 1 was out on $5,000 bail, charged with possessing cocaine. Number 2 was out on $5,000 bail, charged with theft. Number 3 was in for psychiatric observation after he threw two bowling balls through a neighbor's window. Number 4 was criticized for running his campaign from the saloon. Number 5 died after the ballots were printed and it was too late to remove his name. The deceased did pretty well, but lost. The only one of the five to survive the primaries was number 4, the saloon candidate. Democracy is not dead in America.

A word or two about my old friend Benny Goodman, who died on Friday. Of course, everyone knew he was a great clarinet player and led a dance band that played some of the best jazz and swing ever played anywhere. But not so many know he was a piece of American history. He was the first to invite black musicians—and it was their music—to play in a white band. And what made Goodman famous in the first place was the work of a black arranger named Fletcher Henderson. His arrangements were so good Goodman played them for forty years, right up to a week or so before he died. They are now popular classics. And Goodman was the only musician I know of who could play Fletcher Henderson on Monday and Wolfgang Amadeus Mozart on Tuesday. Could and did. A good deal of Henderson's work could be called chamber music. And I believe if Mozart had lived to hear it, he would have liked it.

Next week Congress will be voting to set a new and higher federal government debt limit, to give the Treasury power to borrow still more money. Even though in the last three or four years—if we can believe the claims coming from the White House and Congress—the deficit has been wiped out and there's no need to borrow any more.

In 1981 the White House claimed it had cut $130 billion out of future spending.

In 1982 Congress passed something called the Tax Equity and Fiscal Responsibility Act and claimed it would reduce the deficit by an additional $100 billion.

In 1984 there was the Deficit Reduction Act, claiming to save still another $60 billion.

And a lot of others.

But somehow, the more they've claimed to cut spending, the higher the deficit has risen. It's well over $200 billion a year, every year.

One final note about an election played out almost entirely in thirty-second commercials on television. There was very little handshaking at factory gates, shopping malls or small-town places like Mom's Cafe. Instead, it was all television. A loss.

Here's an example of what we've lost. Years ago John McClellan was running for the Senate in Arkansas. He and his opponent both made speeches from a raised platform at a county fair. His opponent spoke first, blamed McClellan for everything he thought was wrong in the world, got some applause. Then he picked up a water pitcher on the platform's railing to refill his glass. But he was so busy smiling at the crowd he forgot what he was doing and poured the water not in the glass but over the railing and down on the head of a white-haired grandmother in a wheelchair. McClellan waited while people helped her and dried her off and then said to the crowd: "Do you want a senator who's too dumb to pour water in a glass?" He won.

Regrettably, we don't see events like that in thirty-second commercials.

The Republican and Democratic parties are in a dispute unlike those we've all seen and heard for years. This dispute is about the Superdome in New Orleans. The Republicans went down there and made a deal with the city to hold their 1988 presidential nominating convention in the Superdome, on condition that no other party could meet there next year. But the Democrats had been considering New Orleans and asked the Republicans to drop that restriction. They refused.

Here is a suggested solution: the New Orleans Superdome seats 71,330 people, so it's big enough for both parties to meet in it simultaneously. The Republicans could meet at one end of the hall and the Democrats at the other end. They would be able to see and hear each other, from a distance. So if a political speaker at one end of the hall got up to the microphone and made a charge that was a lie—which is not unlikely—the party at the other end could immediately deny it. And at the same time tell another lie of its own. All this should be edifying to the television audience. And if they cooperate just a bit and nominate both presidential candidates on the same night, they could get by with dropping just one shower of balloons. It's such a good idea they won't do it.

We've all been taught honesty is the best policy. Well, a new poll done for *U.S. News & World Report* and CNN shows that 54 percent of the people polled agreed honesty was, in fact, the best. But 54 percent is not exactly an overwhelming vote for honesty. What do the other 46 percent think? We don't know. Furthermore, they were asked what people and professions they trusted the most. They said they trusted television anchorpeople. All right, but they don't deserve much credit for honesty. They don't have any choice. Sixty percent said they trusted their wives and husbands. Only 60 percent. The other 40 percent, I guess, are thought to be like the characters we see in the soap operas—cheating and lying. And, finally, they said they trusted automobile repairmen—40 percent—more than they trusted President Reagan—38 percent. Now, what does that mean? How do they know? How many of them ever had President Reagan fix their carburetors?

It does seem a bit of a shame that Mario Cuomo, after thinking it over, passed up the chance to run for president. It's a shame because he'll miss all the fun. He will miss the excitement of making the same speech—with minor variations—over and over for a year and a half. He will not get to shake hands with all those rich people he may not like very much but has to be nice to because he needs their money. He will not get telephone calls at 5 a.m. from reporters saying something has happened in Outer Mongolia and what does he think about it? It may be he thinks nothing about it, but since he's running for president he has to say something, even if he's not quite sure where Outer Mongolia is. He will not get to go to all the political rallies and fund-raisers at the Howard Johnsons and Holiday Inns, and he will miss eating all the chicken and peas. How could he pass up all of that?

In the nature of their work, airline crews travel from city to city across the country.

This week we learned that one crew member— John Lutter, a flight engineer for United Airlines—flew to a lot of cities, and as he traveled around the country he stopped off long enough to marry one woman after another. One of his wives says he married six different women in six cities from Florida to California and fathered sixteen children. Each wife, she says, thought she was the only one. He told them all he was strictly a one-woman man and they all believed him.

This became known when he disappeared and several of his wives called the police to report him missing. He'd quit his job at United Airlines and disappeared. One of his wives said, "All of us, basically, still love him."

This sounds like a movie script. But if it were made into a movie, would United Airlines ever show it on its planes?

This country was first divided into time zones in the nineteenth century, under pressure from the railroads, who were trying to print timetables. And there are those who still believe we were better off when the railroads ran the country. Anyway, daylight saving time started at 2 a.m. today, early this year because Congress changed the starting date, from the last Sunday in April to the first Sunday. Why? Because of a lobbying campaign by—of all people—the Barbecue Industries Association, manufacturers of all the stuff used for cooking outdoors. Why? Because they think the longer it stays light in the evenings, the more people will cook outside and, of course, use more charcoal. Nobody had any real objection. Congress changed the law. Except in Indiana. The state refuses to go by daylight saving time, but eleven of its counties, scattered around the state, are allowed to observe it if they want to. They do want to. The result is confusion. It is said that a bus rolling over a certain route in Indiana goes through seven time changes in one state. The objections to daylight saving time come from farmers, who work by the sun, not the clock, and call it God's time. Senator Harold Hughes of Iowa, a Bible student, running for reelection, made a speech to a crowd of farmers. They shouted at him: "Why do we need daylight saving time? Why can't we live by God's time?" He answered: "I've studied the Bible all my life and I've never found that God wore a watch."

Increasing numbers of young men and women going to college are studying for M.B.A.'s— Masters in Business Administration. They want to be stockbrokers and investment bankers because they want to make money.

All right, but if they want to make big money they ought to look at these new figures just made public by the Charlotte, North Carolina, *Observer.* They show that the truly big moneymakers are the television evangelists. For example, Jim Bakker and his wife, Tammy. In 1986 they were paid $1,600,000, plus Mercedes cars, lavish houses, gardeners, maids and bodyguards. Until last month they ran a television evangelism program, preaching and saving souls. It is not known exactly how many they saved. But if they saved one a day, with an income of $1,600,000, that works out to $4,383.56 per soul saved.

Can the Harvard Business School match that?

More from the annals of bureaucracy. Over the years I have chronicled more than a few outrages by those on our various public payrolls, and they have ranged from the ridiculous to the hilarious to the stupid. This one is all three. And it happened to me. I received from the District of Columbia tax collector a brisk and officious notice claiming that I owed back taxes from the year 1985. Which I did not. The amount, they said? Ten cents. One dime. It cost them 22 cents to send me the notice. It gets worse. The notice said that unless the 10 cents was paid immediately by certified check, the fines and penalties would be $2,137.32. I've paid the 10 cents, to avoid the hassle of arguing with them. The certified check cost $2.50. With the postage, return receipt and so on, the 10 cents I did not owe cost me about $4.00. A $2,000 fine for claimed back taxes of 10 cents? That's the law, they said. That concludes today's lesson in democracy in action.

If anyone still thinks this is not a crazy world, look at this.

In 1945, during World War II, there was an Army captain in California named Ronald Reagan. He was turning out public relations movies and still pictures for the military. He ordered an Army photographer to go out and take some pictures of women doing war work. The photographer found a young woman working in a factory making communications gear; she was quite attractive and her name was Norma Jean Dougherty. He took twenty-five pictures of her. They were so well received she left the factory and changed her name to Marilyn Monroe.

The rest, as they say, is history. Until this week. The same twenty-five pictures turned up for sale at Christie's auction house in London. They were sold for $23,000.

Among the presidential candidates, there's a good deal of talk today about Senator Joseph Biden's making a speech he borrowed from Neil Kinnock, head of Britain's Labour party, who lost the last election. Biden repeated, almost word for word, a Kinnock speech asking why he was the first in his family ever to go to college and noting that his ancestors had been coal miners and never had a chance. The first accusation was that Biden was guilty of plagiarism, stealing Kinnock's words and passing them off as his own. But it appears he did credit Kinnock, several times.

But that's the wrong question. The right question is, if he's going to borrow a campaign speech, why borrow one from a loser?

If that's what Biden wants, he could go back into the files and borrow Walter Mondale's campaign speech promising to raise taxes. Or Gerald Ford's famous speech saying the Russians did not dominate Eastern Europe.

There's plenty of this stuff around and there's no need to steal it from the British.

The oldest news ever on this program—3,500 years old. That was when Daedalus, a Greek inventor, flew from Crete across the open sea to his home on the Greek mainland. He used birds' feathers and wax to make two sets of wings, one for himself and one for his son Icarus. They took off, wings flapping. Daedalus made it home. Icarus flew too high, too close to the sun, the heat melted the wax, and his wings came apart. He fell into the sea, never to be seen again. A pity.

Last week a Greek athlete made the same trip in a tiny foot-powered airplane. He flew 74 miles over the open sea at about 18 miles an hour and arrived safely.

This information is offered as a suggestion to all those Americans standing around the airports wondering how to get home when the airlines cancel their flights.

In Moscow next month, at the big Communist party conference, 5,000 delegates will gather to talk about their political system.

And now on Moscow radio there has been a proposal that the conference be covered on live television, like the American conventions of the Democratic and Republican parties coming up this summer. A fine idea, but the Russians have absolutely no experience in doing this, while all of us here have a great deal of experience. And so a few words of free advice on how to do it.

First, they need a Sam Donaldson who will roam through the crowds on the floor with a microphone, asking questions they don't want to answer.

And they need a George Will who will watch intently from a glassed-in booth and then go on television with critical comments they do not want to hear.

Plus, of course, a lot of politicians experienced in spending thirty minutes to make five-minute speeches. If they don't have enough of these, they could borrow some of ours. We have plenty.

Even better, if Gorbachev feels all this is too

much for him to handle, they could just bring the whole party conference here to this country and let us do it for them.

Everyone Is Entitled to My Opinion

Every four years the politicians close the doors, take pen in hand and do a little creative writing, turning out documents called party platforms. This is going on now.

The Republican platform will say whatever George Bush wants it to say, since he is without opposition. The Democratic platform will say whatever Michael Dukakis wants that Jesse Jackson will accept. The two documents, then, will be two sets of promises, saying in effect, "Folks, elect us and this is what we'll do."

But in truth it's not that neat. Instead of promises, the platforms should say: "This is what we think will attract some votes, and sometime, maybe, we'll even do it, if we can get the votes in Congress, if we can find the money, if there's not too much public complaint, and unless we learn in the meantime it won't work."

A platform, then, is a campaign document not unlike a thirty-second television commercial. Longer, yes, but just as fleeting.

The networks are concerned because the movie and television writers are on strike and not turning out scripts for new programs for the fall. And the networks are worried they'll have to fill the whole season with reruns.

There is a solution. Forget Hollywood. Washington is full of the kind of material the networks have been paying for, and it's all free. That is, material about money, power, greed, sex, corruption—it's all here.

Hustlers on the telephone happily discussing their kickbacks and bribes from defense contractors while the FBI sits listening and running tape recorders.

A congressman from Ohio keeping on his office payroll a young woman listed as a typist but who can't type a line.

A candidate for president out on a yacht with a model.

A member of Congress having his office staff write a book with his name on it and then selling a thousand copies to the Teamsters Union, not previously known for its literary interests.

Can the Hollywood writers do better than that? No.

Richard Nixon was at the White House Friday for a private talk with the president. They still consult him.

Nixon, of course, is a unique figure in American politics. He's been in Congress, served as vice president twice and was a candidate for president three times—elected twice, almost impeached once, resigned once and pardoned once.

Politically, then, he has nothing left to lose or to gain. And so he is well situated to perform one final service for his country—as the Official U.S. Government Scapegoat. This would be a new office in the White House basement. The holder would get a chauffeured limousine with red lights on it, a police escort and his own engraved stationery. His duty would be to take the blame for everything that goes wrong.

If Nixon held this office now, George Bush would not have to claim he had never heard of the Iran arms deal. He could simply say it was Dick Nixon's fault, and Nixon would step forward and say yes, I did it.

It would put into the system what politicians in both parties have always wanted—to take the credit for successes and to dump the blame for failure on somebody else.

If these politicians are as smart as they say, how come I had to figure this out?

Somebody on the staff of the House Ways and Means Committee has come up with a new and profoundly silly idea for squeezing another dollar or two out of the taxpayers.

The new regulation is this: people who work at home and who deduct as a business expense a portion of their family's telephone bills may not include in their deductions any part of the $10 or $12 basic monthly charge for the phone.

This will not pay off the federal debt. It may not pay the salary of whoever thought it up. And it likely won't even pay for the paper the new regulation is printed on.

Congress does indeed pay people to sit around thinking up ideas as annoying and silly as that. They might do better to be out doing something useful, like mowing the Capitol lawn, or washing cars.

We've just heard what President Reagan will do when he leaves the White House. Just for the record, here's what some other presidents did when they left. Harry Truman, after watching President Eisenhower get sworn in at the U.S. Capitol, rode about three blocks to the railroad station and took the first train back to Missouri. Thomas Jefferson retired to Monticello, his house in Virginia, founded the University of Virginia, read the Greek and Roman histories, sold his books to the U.S. government for what became the Library of Congress and died broke. George Washington returned to Mount Vernon for what he said would give him more enjoyment than of all of his forty years in public life. Teddy Roosevelt left for Africa and spent ten months in the jungle killing animals. And Gerald Ford, on his first day out of the White House, flew to California to play in the Bing Crosby Pro Am golf tournament at Pebble Beach.

February 12, 1989

Representative Wayne Hays of Ohio died this week. Predictably, the reports of his death dwelled on his affair with Elizabeth Ray, a young woman he kept on his office payroll as a typist, even though she couldn't type a line. That was the gossipy news years ago. But the real news was that Hays—unknown to the public—had enormous power. He was chairman of the Administration Committee, in charge of House members' perks, which are numerous, including free parking in the House garage. One day there was a disagreement—the nature of it is lost to history—that dragged on and on and neither side would give in. Finally, Hays said, "Leave this to me." He took one of the arguing groups into another office, closed the door, and in about three minutes they came out and said it was all settled. Later, he was asked: "How did you do that?" He said, "I told them if they didn't come around they'd find their parking spaces moved a mile away. They turned white and instantly agreed." In Washington, that's power.

I am pleased to report there is one more thing we don't have to worry about. The Internal Revenue Service has sent a report to professionals in the tax field—those who have to know about things like this—saying that in the event of war and nuclear attack on this country, the collection of taxes will continue. It says that within thirty days after the last nuclear blast, the IRS will be all set up to assess, collect and record tax payments, and will be ready to issue, as necessary, new forms and regulations concerning how to keep your taxes paid during the emergency. It says in the areas of this country hardest hit, delinquent taxpayers will be given a little extra time. Otherwise, taxes will be collected as usual. For those who have worried about this—if there are any—who have wondered whether in a nuclear attack there would be anyone there to accept their tax payments, the answer, they say, is yes, the IRS will be there.

Some interesting—and unsettling—figures this week from the U.S. Bureau of the Census. It reports that governments—federal, state and local—now have more people on their payrolls than ever before in history—more than 17 million. This should not surprise anyone, since we have known that government agencies always want larger budgets and longer payrolls, and usually get them. What is startling is this: in government employment all over the United States, the fastest-growing job category is prison guard.

The more criminals we lock up, the more guards we need to stand over them with guns to stop them from hacksawing through the iron bars or climbing out through the air shafts. So these jobs represent new career opportunities for young men and women attracted to this kind of work, government's fastest-growing field of employment.

In Moscow this week we saw how far glasnost has gone. Pretty far. We've all seen the news pictures of two world statesmen speaking different languages and talking to each other with a faceless, expressionless translator standing between them. And when the translator hears state secrets, he's expected to keep them secret—if he knows what's good for him. Now a Russian who translated for Joseph Stalin revealed some of those secrets on Russian television. For one, he said Stalin admired Adolf Hitler, spoke well of him. And when he heard that Hitler had murdered the entire leadership of his storm troopers, the SA, Stalin said fine, that's how to deal with political enemies. Kill them.

Another little piece of history: at their famous meeting in Yalta, President Roosevelt and Stalin had a private meeting with a translator present taking notes. Later, Roosevelt said to Stalin that their conversation would be deeply embarrassing if the translator's notes ever became public. Shortly, Stalin sent Roosevelt a message: the notes had been burned and the translator had been shot.

One of the week's news events: a New York court found Leona Helmsley—who advertises herself as the queen guarding her hotels—guilty on thirty-three charges of tax cheating. Of evading $1,200,000 in federal income taxes.

It was the nuttiest piece of news of the summer. The charge was that she bought personal items for the Helmsleys' country mansion in Connecticut and charged them to their hotels in New York, calling them tax deductions. Such items as a bug zapper for $32. And a year's membership in a crossword-puzzle club for $21. These and other more expensive items, they said, saved her and her husband $1,200,000 in taxes.

But the Helmsleys are worth several billions, and a million or so means nothing to them. And in the same years she was accused of evading $1,200,000, they paid $57,800,000. Paying $57 million and then maybe going to jail for not paying $1 million more? Is this arrogance on the part of a woman who calls herself the queen? Or simple stupidity?

In either case, if she goes to jail, she will then have time to work all those crossword puzzles.

The Soviet Union may not be ready for this. Boris Yeltsin, a member of the Soviet Parliament and the member most popular with the public, says Gorbachev isn't doing enough and isn't doing it fast enough, that he's too careful and too cautious. Now Yeltsin has arrived in the United States. In Washington this week, he says he wants to study the workings of the United States Congress. Which may be all right, but given the present state of the Soviet economy, they can't possibly afford a Congress like ours. And it's not clear that we can either. But beyond that, Yeltsin has been booked for nine lectures in nine big American cities—New York, Baltimore, Washington, Chicago, Dallas, Miami and others. Nine lectures, each paying a fee of $25,000. That's $225,000 in all.

Now, this is something new in Soviet-American relations and it does raise interesting possibilities. Suppose we invited all the members of the Soviets' Politburo over here and sent them across this country giving nine or ten lectures for $25,000 each, and sent them home rich, since

American dollars are worth a good deal more in Moscow than they're worth here.

Could this be a way to end the cold war? If so, it certainly would be the cheapest way.

One more word about the schools, and a note from small-town America. Every presidential election year, New Hampshire has the first primary and the politicians pour into the state, the press along with them. Soon there will be the familiar news report that New Hampshire has no state income tax and no sales tax, and therefore spends less money on its schools than some other states. It is taken for granted, of course, that this is bad, but if one talks to the teachers it appears it's not so bad.

For one reason, the state keeps its educational bureaucracy small, while in some other states the administrators threaten to outnumber the students. For another, a teacher said they didn't need so much money because they get help from home. For example, he said, if he wants to take thirty students to visit an art gallery, he sends the word out and the next morning there will be ten parents in their cars lined up at school ready to drive the students to the gallery and bring them back.

That kind of help and support may be worth more than money.

This may not be the world's most important news, but perhaps it should not pass unnoticed. Jim Bakker, the television evangelist, went to prison this week, in Minnesota. He will be put to work in the prison mess hall, cleaning tables and washing pots and pans. And the former multi-millionaire television preacher will be paid 11 cents an hour. It may be that this will build character. At about the same time, another celebrated defendant—Zsa Zsa Gabor—was found guilty of slapping a policeman and sentenced to do a little time behind bars. Three days.

It has been suggested that the two of them be locked up in the same cell. But prison authorities, lacking romantic and poetic imagination, will not do it.

One more note about drugs. In September, President Bush made a speech about the dangers of drugs, and he held up a bag of cocaine and said it had been bought from a drug dealer just across the street from the White House. It was. But he didn't tell the whole story. The federal drug agent they sent to make the buy had nothing but trouble. He asked a dealer he knew to meet him in the park across the street from the White House. He didn't show up because he didn't know where the White House was. They had to bring him over. The federal drug agent had a microphone concealed under his shirt to make tapes for evidence in court. But the microphone failed to work. And he had a cameraman standing back out of sight to make a videotape of the drug transaction, also for evidence in court. But he got no pictures because just as the sale was about to be made, he was mugged.

Life in Washington.

A few months ago there were thirteen Communist countries in the world. Now, an eventful few months later, we have five: the Soviet Union, China, Cuba, South Yemen and North Korea. North Korea may be the most stubborn and hard-line of all of them. It shows no interest in any change at all. And it goes on glowering in hatred across its borders with South Korea. But now this: it has been discovered that North Korea has been digging tunnels under the border, 400 and 500 feet below ground, under the border into South Korea. The tunnels are 6 feet high and 6 feet wide, big enough for soldiers to march through, three abreast. And the idea, South Korea says, is to invade the south through the tunnels.

The following advice is offered, free of charge, to the South Korean military: if North Korea invades and begins marching its troops to the south, 400 and 500 feet underground, wait until the tunnels are jammed with troops and then pump them full of water. If we have five Communist countries now, then we'd have four.

In the movie industry it is commonly said that the most creative writing in Hollywood is done not by the screenwriters but by the bookkeepers. According to the figures they put out, hardly any movie ever makes a profit. If one threatens to show a profit, they will look around for new expenses to load on and make the profit disappear.

But now my friend Art Buchwald is suing Paramount Pictures, saying they used a film idea of his without credit and that he's therefore entitled to a percentage of the profit from a movie that brought in $125 million. Paramount says yes, it did take in $125 million gross, but after all the deductions there's no profit.

An income of $125 million, and the books show it all disappeared and there's no profit? That certainly requires great creativeness.

Considering how well they do this, it might be a good idea to bring Hollywood's bookkeepers here to Washington, turn them loose on the federal deficit and see if they can make that disappear.

Nothing else works.

On the first Earth Day twenty years ago, I was in England, where I found a beautiful little village—thatched roofs, green meadows with sheep, flowers everywhere. The road into the town was lined on both sides with enormous oak trees, three hundred years old, they said. The County Council recently had told the village that the road into town was too narrow for modern traffic and had to be widened. But to widen the road they'd have to cut down the oak trees. The village said absolutely not. You will not cut down our trees. They argued and argued and finally reached a compromise: the county could plant two new rows of trees 30 feet farther apart than the old ones, and when the new trees reached the same size as the old ones, in maybe two hundred years, or three hundred, then they could cut the old trees and widen the road. That was the deal they made. So the oaks will be cut and the road widened in about two hundred years from now. Who says we can't save the environment?

A familiar piece of news this week: a tanker in the Gulf of Mexico spilling oil. Familiar, yes, because every week or two there's a tanker somewhere fouling the water. At this moment, a spill in the inland waters between New York and New Jersey, in the same place where in recent weeks there have been four oil spills. Four. Why is this? The ships don't spill American grain on its way to Russia. They don't spill Japanese cars, stereos and computers crossing the Pacific to the United States. They don't spill the bananas coming up here from Central America. They don't spill the passengers on those cruise ships we see in the television commercials, singing about how much fun they're having. During World War II the ships hauled entire American armies and their supplies across the Atlantic without losing a single soldier's life. Now, if my count is correct, there have been sixteen oil spills in a few months, not counting the big one in Alaska. Why can't they move oil without spilling it? What's the matter with you guys?

In Congress this week, an interesting laboratory study of Washington at its worst, and best. There was a vote in the House on amending the Constitution's Bill of Rights to prohibit desecration of the American flag. They wondered: how could anyone vote against protecting the flag and have any hope of reelection in a country that reveres it? But they raised another question. The Bill of Rights is one of the grandest documents in human history. It has kept this country free. Who wants to mess around with that? So it was a choice between protecting the flag and protecting the Constitution—a political question raw and mean and close to the bone.

In their debate they talked of how a vote against the amendment would look in the next election in flag-waving thirty-second commercials on television. A congresswoman from Ohio said she had stayed up the night before the vote reading the Bill of Rights and a biography of Patrick Henry. A member from Nebraska said he didn't want his tombstone to say he voted to weaken the Constitution.

When it was all over, after the members had

gone home, the House chamber had been vacu-
umed and the lights turned out, the flag could
still be burned, but the Constitution was intact.

I see in *The New York* Times that the American people have become increasingly irritated with pollsters, surveyors and salesmen calling them on the phone. So irritated at these intrusions on their privacy that more and more of them simply refuse to talk. The *Times* quotes a Mrs. Oliva in California who said, "It was seven o'clock, I was trying to get the kids to bed, it was zoo time around here, and that's when these people call. I don't want to spend time talking to them." Telephone solicitors call around six or seven because that's when most people are home. But it's also the time when most people are busy with children, cooking, eating, tuning into the news, and don't want to talk to pollsters asking how they plan to vote in the election for mayor, sheriff and water commissioner. In the Northeast, 49 percent of those answering refused to talk and slammed down the phone. It's surprising that telephone solicitors don't just give up. How can you sell anything when you call at six or seven, get somebody out of the bathtub, dripping wet, the dog barking, the baby crying, the doorbell ringing, and you ask: "Pardon me, but do you own a vacuum cleaner?"

When Congress adjourned and went home, it left the new tax bill lying there like a mulch pile, and people are still digging through it and finding nasty little lumps nobody knew were there. Such as this: the old tax law says a baby, on reaching two years of age, must have a Social Security number to put on his Form 1040 when he pays his taxes. That's two years old. The new law? In an act of statesmanship, courage and fiscal responsibility, it changes the rule to apply to babies one year old. This must be an example of the fairness the Democrats keep talking about. It means all those babies rolling around in their cribs and playing with rattles will have to pay taxes like the rest of us. Will the waiting rooms at H & R Block's tax offices be filled with baby carriages and strollers? Will Block keep a supply of diapers for those in need? Will Congress in next year's tax bill require Social Security numbers within one minute of birth so if there is any money they can get it and spend it sooner? Can the U.S. Congress be silly? Yes. Very.

In Washington this week Margaret Thatcher, Britain's retired prime minister, made a luncheon speech. Now, the Washington luncheon speech, usually in a hotel ballroom, is a familiar art form, its structure honed and polished over hundreds of speeches delivered over thousands of plates of chicken and peas. The first rule seems to be this: say nothing new and nothing interesting. Perhaps because at lunchtime, when the chicken is eaten, people are eager to get out and back to work.

But Margaret Thatcher violated the rule. About the war in the Gulf, she said: "Only one nation really has the power to defend freedom in the world. That is now and in the foreseeable future, the United States." Having thought about American history more than most Americans have, she said: "European nations are not and never will be like this. They are the product of their history. While America is a product of philosophy." Or, history created Europe. America was created by Americans.

Not the usual Washington luncheon speech.

We see in the full-page newspaper ads that the airlines are offering cut-price fares, sort of. From this town to that for $86, or another town for $112. But what is all that fine print down at the bottom of the ad? Here's what it says. Listen carefully.

Twenty-five percent off all published round-trip fares of $200 or more available at time of reservations for which passenger qualifies. Reservations must be made and tickets purchased per the rule of the fare used. However, all tickets must be purchased by April 12. Nonrefundable. Sunday night stay-over is required. All other rules and restrictions of the published fare will also apply. All travel must originate on or after April 1 and be completed by June 15, or per the fare used, whichever occurs first. Coupon is not valid with MCOs, PTAs, teletickets, tickets by mail or any other certificate, coupon or promotional offer, and so on.

There's much more, but I've run out of time. If you want to fly somewhere and try to read all this junk first, you'll miss the plane.

The following may not leave a dry eye in the house. Not long ago Kuwait was a collection of mud huts. Then Americans came in and found that it was sitting on a pool of oil. The money poured in. The Kuwaitis made sure to keep it all for themselves. They set up a register, or list, which they still keep, of what they call real Kuwaitis—that is, those with Kuwaiti parents and grandparents. They are the only ones allowed to live permanently in the country. Others could come in and work, but they couldn't buy houses or any real estate. They could only rent. And at age sixty-five, they had to leave the country. This way, every Kuwaiti household kept a staff of servants, who did the cooking and cleaning. And around the country they cleaned the streets, collected the garbage and so on. Now, with the war, the outside workers have left. The country is in such chaos they can't work. The Kuwaitis find they've depended on foreign workers so long they hardly know how to do anything themselves. When it comes to rebuilding the country, one is inclined to ask: "Who will do the work?" A good question.

In about the year 1300, the poet Dante thought the earth would end in fire and ice, a prediction still remembered. But as famous as Dante's poetic line has remained, it now appears to be wrong. The *New England Journal of Medicine* reports that the cost of health care in this country—government and private—has climbed to $666 billion a year. And about 35 million Americans have to pay these costs out of their pockets, if they can, because they have no health insurance. What the *Journal* also reports is that of this $666 billion for health care, a fourth of it is spent not on doctors, nurses, hospitals or medication, but on paperwork. About a fourth. If the paperwork could be cut in half, it would save enough money to buy health insurance for all 35 million Americans who are without it. And then everyone would be insured. But Washington loves paperwork. Cannot get enough of it. So, on this point, Dante was wrong. The world will not end in fire and ice. It will drown in paper.

For five years southern California has had either no rain or not enough rain, and so it had to put restrictions on the use of water. The Los Angeles water department asked people to cut down their use of water by 15 percent. They responded splendidly. They cut back by 30 percent. The water department said "Hold on, that's too much!" With the use of water dropping by 30 percent, the department wasn't collecting enough in water bills to pay for its operations, and has gone $13 million in the hole. So the department says it can't afford to have people saving this much water and if they keep it up it will have to raise its rates. Crazy, yes. But there it is.

From Los Angeles, a few facts—from *Los Angeles Magazine*—showing how this city ranks compared with other American cities.

Close to number one in terms of climate and sunny days a year.

Number one in car telephones.

Number one for good-looking women and good-looking men. Possibly because it's number one in cosmetic surgeons—289.

And it's number one in hairdressing salons for dogs—14, including one called the Bowser Boutique.

And, of course, number one in traffic congestion.

On that point, a report I read here: a man driving along a Los Angeles freeway in a camper, one of those fixed up inside with beds, a kitchen, bathroom and so on. He ran into a traffic jam and couldn't move for half an hour. While he sat there, there was a knock on the camper's door. It was a man from three cars back asking if he could come in and use the bathroom.

We've all seen the pictures over the years of the British royal family carrying out their civic duties by appearing at ceremonial occasions, cutting ribbons to open new hotels and museums, visiting schools and so on.

And when one of the royals is scheduled to appear, there's always quite a lot of fluttering around, dusting, polishing the doorknobs and making sure everything is perfectly in order.

But here's a new one. Princess Diana, in Canada, visited the Ontario Museum of Nature, where everything was immaculate. From there, she was scheduled to visit a new hospital heart clinic. While the staff was bustling about and getting everything in order, they noticed that a great many of the hospital beds were empty. They thought that wouldn't look right. So what did they do? They rounded up a lot of perfectly healthy people and asked them to climb into the beds and look sick.

The princess never noticed.

Why did President Bush get sick in Tokyo? This must have had something to do with it:

He left Washington, flew to Texas, hunted quail by day and ate barbecue by night and drank beer in a dance hall.

Then a ten-hour flight to Hawaii, two miles of jogging before another nine hours to Australia and then into a boat to watch fireworks. In the morning, jogging again, shaking hands and signing autographs.

Then to Canberra for ceremonies, back south to Melbourne, then back north to hot, steamy Singapore. A press conference in the tropical sun, two speeches, a visit to a school and a state dinner.

Then to Seoul, South Korea, where it was freezing. To the tennis court. Next, breakfast with businessmen, meetings, a joint press conference, a speech to the National Assembly. And a visit to the American troops and back to Seoul for a state dinner.

In Japan, from the Osaka airport by helicopter to Kyoto and some kind of game called *kemari.* Now a visit to the ancient throne room, where he looked as if he'd like to sit on it. He opened a toy store, took a helicopter back to Osaka and then flew to Tokyo, where at dinner he passed out.

Not surprising he passed out. It was surprising that he got up.

Two striking events in the week's news. One was that Presidents Bush and Yeltsin went to Camp David and had a cozy time sitting around the stone fireplace. They discussed the future and announced that—formally and officially—the cold war was over. And that their two countries hereafter will be friends and will begin destroying the nuclear weapons that have terrified the world for forty years. That was one event. The other was that a supermarket tabloid, the *Star,* quoted a part-time nightclub singer as saying she'd had an affair with Governor Bill Clinton, now running for president. The governor denied it.

Which of these two events got the most publicity in this country? The sexy scandal, of course. Supermarkets promise that their food is clean and wholesome. They make no such claim for their tabloids. So why do they put them right at the checkout line beside the cash register? Why don't they put them in the back of the store among the mops and brooms and paper towels?

President Bush in his State of the Union speech said he would order a stop, for a limited time, to the issuing of new government regulations. There are so many of these that a government newspaper called the *Federal Register* prints nothing but new rules and regulations. Why Mr. Bush stopped it temporarily was not clear, but it is clear that manufacturers complain they are drenched, drowned in a constant flood of new regulations, each one requiring another label, another sticker, another warning. A quick count in one bathroom found fifty warnings, some of them useful and necessary, some quite silly.

Because of overeager regulators, who apparently find some pleasure in it, the *Federal Register* bulges. It includes such warnings as a label on paint cans saying "Do not drink paint." And a label on an electric hair dryer saying "Do not use while sleeping."

What would we do without Washington to look after us?

March 8, 1992

One of the U.S. government's favorite pastimes is tapping people's telephones. It keeps a fair number of people busy and working and drawing salaries. Most of what they hear is extremely boring. If they take any notes, they go into the files and in most cases stay there forever, unread.

Now, however, wiretapping is no longer so easy. The telephone systems are changing over from copper wires to fiber optics capable of carrying hundreds of calls on one cable, and to separate out an individual call requires complicated technology.

The U.S. Department of Justice, which does seem to have too many lawyers, is asking Congress for money in order that the phone companies can modify their systems so they can still be tapped. And—no surprise—it wants to put the cost on your and my telephone bill.

Only a pack of bureaucrats could think that up. The only thing worse would be their cutting in on your phone call and saying, "Excuse me, but I'm a government agent tapping your phone and making notes. Would you mind speaking a little more slowly?"

March 15, 1992

The *New York Times* reports that for a good long time, the House of Representatives bank has been seen as a good place to pick up a little money in time of need, no questions asked.

In 1947, the House Sergeant-at-Arms, in charge of the bank, made off with $143,000, invested in Florida real estate, lost it and spent a year in prison.

But long before that, in 1889, a cashier in the House bank left Washington. He took with him a suitcase containing the entire payroll of the House of Representatives, which was $75,000, equal to about a million dollars today.

He also took with him his very, very close friend, a local prostitute named Lulu. The two of them fled to Canada with the money and were never seen again.

Jerry Brown still pushes the flat tax. The Republicans wrote their tax bill and the Democratic Congress voted it down. The Democrats wrote theirs and the Republican president vetoed it. So it goes in election years, tinkering with the tax code and usually winding up making it worse, if that's possible. Worse in the sense of making it even more complicated and even more incomprehensible. The tax bill that came out of the Senate Finance Committee a short time ago runs on for 800 pages and here's a sample of its language (which may be English but I'm not sure):

Subparagraph B in section 1 G 7, relating to income included on parents' return, is amended (1) by striking $1,000 in clause i and inserting twice the amount described in paragraph 4 A ii I and (2) by amending subclause II of clause ii to read as follows . . . And so on.

The proper place for this is not in a tax law nobody can understand. The only place for it is in the nearest sanitary landfill. Why do we have to put up with this stuff?

It was T. B. Macaulay who said, "We know no spectacle as ridiculous as the British public in one of its periodic fits of morality."

Today he might say the same about Washington. Since the rubber-check scandal, some of the politicians here are scared half to death they will be voted out of office. We halfway expect to see some of them sitting around red-eyed, crying into damp handkerchiefs. They fear losing their seats and some of their privileges and perks, and now they're doing away with one perk after another, hoping it's not too late.

The secretary of state, who's not even elected, decided this week it was too expensive to travel on military planes. So when on personal errands he may be seen flying commercial, coach class. That's where the airlines serve what they call a snack—something like an apple, a few crackers and a little foil sack with twelve peanuts in it.

It's a good thing John Sununu left the government when he did. One as sybaritic, pampered and luxury-loving as he is would not have stood for this, suffering for his country in coach class eating peanuts.

April 19, 1992

The Speaker of the House, Representative Tom Foley of Washington, trying to put the rubber-check scandal behind him, says he thinks it's been overblown. Evidence from around the country suggests that people think it's under-blown, if that's a word; that the political damage is even worse than the House leadership seems to think.

Either way, across the country candidates for election or reelection are practically prostrating themselves before the voters and begging forgiveness. Some blame the bank for sloppy record-keeping, some blame their wives for writing checks and not telling them. Others—somewhat more romantic—say they were so drained by their duties at the altar of public service they were just too tired to balance their checkbooks.

How many of those excuses, if any, would be accepted in an audit by the IRS?

It is our policy to keep you up-to-date on the events and nonevents in the world of politics. Over recent years we've all seen or suffered through great numbers of thirty-second political commercials. In politics, they have become the basic American art form, if you want to call them that. People have built their careers and put their kids through college by learning how to squeeze the maximum number of insults into exactly thirty seconds.

Now the news: in California, where television airtime is expensive and people are sick of listening to politicians anyway, the new thing is the ten-second commercial. The cost for the airtime is half as much, and it is said that brevity is the soul of wit anyway. They can say a lot in ten seconds. For example, how about this?

My opponent is a liar and a thief who talks one way and votes another. He is eight months behind in his alimony. And not only that, when he was eighteen years old he smoked pot, and he *did* inhale.

Ten seconds.

A small note in the news. Very small. Size 5 1/2, to be exact.

Imelda Marcos, the no doubt grieving widow of Ferdinand Marcos, the late president of the Philippines, believes her husband had more money than she has been able to find. Some thievery somewhere, maybe. So she's roaming around the Pacific looking for the money she believes he put away somewhere out of sight—in an obscure bank, a safe deposit box or someplace.

This week she went to Hong Kong, a big financial center, and looked around for his money—a few million, she hoped. She found no money. But, to nobody's surprise, in Hong Kong she did find some shoes, just her size—5 1/2. She bought several thousand dollars' worth of them.

Her husband is gone and she can't find his money, but she did find what is for her the next best thing—new shoes.

Local governments around the country are moaning and groaning that they're financially strapped—partly because Washington used to give them money in the form of grants but now keeps most of the money itself. Local taxes have risen so high it's politically difficult to raise them any further. But officials claim they have to get more money from somewhere. So how about this?

Here in Washington, the city collects $50 million a year from parking and traffic tickets—speeding, overtime parking and so on. Fifty million a year, but it's not enough, and so we had this little episode. A traffic policeman was standing on the curb ticketing a car that was illegally parked. While he was writing, a thief came up with a screwdriver and stole the car's license plate. The policeman watched, waited, did nothing and then wrote out another ticket for driving a car without a license plate.

In South Florida, they're selling T-shirts bearing the picture not of a politician, not of Ludwig von Beethoven and not even of a movie star, but a picture of a local television weatherman, Bryan Norcross, who became a hero during the agony of Hurricane Andrew. A woman in Hollywood, Florida, said, "God knows how many lives he saved. He was calm, he was cool, he was fantastic." The Miami *Herald* said, "Where would South Florida have been without him?"

What he did was to stay on the air twenty-two hours straight, warning people that the hurricane was going to be a bad one, and that the safest place in the house is inside a closet, or in a bathtub—advice to people who had never seen a hurricane before. Norcross's boss, the television station manager, Dick Lobo, said he was the voice of authority and strength on that horrendous night, but he's no matinee idol. Says Lobo: "He's got a raspy, high-pitched voice and on the air he blinks a lot."

Mr. Lobo, everybody blinks a lot.

If Clinton wins he will have no problem with housing when he moves to Washington. He will live in the White House, free. And Vice President Gore will live in the vice president's mansion on Massachusetts Avenue, free.

But what about his Cabinet and staff and others who move here from Little Rock, Arkansas? In Little Rock the median price for a house is $69,000. In the Washington area the median price is $159,000—more than twice as much as in Little Rock.

And the sad fact, the nasty little surprise that awaits them, is that the parts of town they will want to live in cost not twice as much as in Little Rock, but three or four times as much, and more. No government job pays money like that. And the Washington city income tax is about the highest in the country.

So some may do what I have known others to do in the past: come to town for a government job, look at the after-tax paycheck, consider the cost of housing and everything else, and decide to turn around and go back home.

December 6, 1992

The Somali operation by U.S. military forces gives new meaning to the word bizarre. American troops going halfway around the world to help in the feeding of people starving to death when there is food but their own leaders won't let them have it. Who instead sit back and let their own forces steal it. Nonstop looting.

To stop this, the U.S. military has had to move into a place with no government, no electricity, no drinking water, inadequate ports and airfields, no housing—nowhere to sleep but on the ground. They must arrange to refuel airplanes in midair all the way from the West Coast of the United States, and must bring in trucks, construction equipment and bulldozers to make the ports and airfields usable and to carry in everything they will need in a place that has nothing.

And all this with no assurance that when they leave, things will be any better. Who else could do all this? Who else would?

Everyone Is Entitled to My Opinion

In Washington, power is everything—not love, not money—but power. But unless you're elected or appointed to some office, your only source of power will be what you know. And so it's thought to be unwise to be caught not knowing something.

This week, a New York magazine called *Spy,* which likes to play pranks on public figures, telephoned several members of Congress new in Washington, said that they were on a call-in radio program and had a few questions.

One was: "Do you approve of what this country is doing to stop what is going on in Freedonia?"

Of course, there is no Freedonia. It was a joke in an old Marx Brothers movie. But a new Congress member from Florida answered the question and said, "Yes, I approve. These situations are very sad." And a new member from Indiana said "Yes, I approve. This is different from the Middle East." And so on.

They soon learn to get out of traps like this. If you don't know the answer, be evasive. Say something like, "I won't decide on that until I read the commitee report." There is no commitee report, but nobody knows it.

The worst and most damaging answer is "I don't know."

As we all know, every federal, state, county and city government is always looking for ways to squeeze more money out of the taxpayers. This city, Washington, is no different. It looks with envy at New York's commuter tax. Those who work in New York and live in other states pay income tax on what they earn in New York.

Washington is a small federal district surrounded by Maryland and Virginia and a metropolitan area of about 4 million people. Thousands of them flood into the city in the morning, work here all day and leave at night, paying their income taxes to the states where they live. Washington wants a commuter tax like New York's, but Congress still has to approve the city's budget and it won't allow it. So a few city officials are discussing another idea: put a gate at every entrance to the city and charge a toll to come in.

It's a cute idea, but people come in to work by car, bus, train, subway, and even a few on the Potomac River in boats. Cars they can stop and collect tolls. But how about those traveling underground on the subway? Would they go down there, stop the trains and go through the passengers' pockets? And those who come in boats? Will the city have a Navy to prevent tax-dodging on the river? Have they thought this through?

Everyone Is Entitled to My Opinion

President Clinton talks of sacrifice; he advocates it, apparently seeing it as a cleansing, purifying experience, good for the soul. Also, it's supposed to save money. If it does, it will be a new and highly unwelcome experience for the U.S. government.

One example: the newly appointed secretary of housing and urban development took over his new agency, looked around and discovered it had $11 billion 100 million lying around unspent, unused for months. Obviously there was no urgent need for it.

There's a lot of argument about this now. But in a new administration calling for sacrifices, cutting government payrolls, raising taxes, what might they do with the $11 billion? Put it back in the Treasury?

Don't count on it.

A few words on how to get a job in the Clinton administration at a time when there are more than a thousand eager job-seekers standing around, waiting. All of them have some reason to believe they might be appointed to something. Some have political connections, some are old friends of the Clintons, and some have expertise in fields where the government will need help.

The first rule is, of course, well known: don't hire any illegal aliens, taxes paid or not. What was common practice in Washington for years is now unacceptable. If you've hired them in the past, even years ago, the White House will find it out, so look for a job somewhere else.

Being a genius will not necessarily be held against you so long as you keep quiet about it. Remember John Sununu? He boasted about how smart he was, proving he was not very smart. So he was fired.

Again, if you can't find a legal American, wash the dishes, cut the grass, run the vacuum and look after the children yourself. It's important.

March 14, 1993

To deal with the famine in Somalia, the United States and the United Nations sent in food to feed the hungry.

Thugs and thieves began stealing the donated food, selling it to those who had money, leaving the poor to starve. The U.S. sent in the United States Marines to stop the stealing and to see that the food went to those in need. They succeeded. The food is getting around. The hungry are being fed.

Now Somalia's leaders complain bitterly that all the free food pouring in from the outside is flooding the market and driving local farmers out of business. With all the free food around, the farmers can't sell anything.

Sometimes you can't win.

We don't do book plugs, but this is a book plug of sorts. It's a paperback and the title is *The 776 Stupidest Things Ever Said.* Here are a few sample quotes:

Movie actor George Raft in a telegram to a producer: "You say this picture deal will be 50/50. In fact it will be the reverse."

A councilman from the District of Columbia: "If crime went down 100 percent it would still be fifty times higher than it should be."

Frank Rizzo, former mayor of Philadelphia: "The streets of this city are safe. It's only the people who make them unsafe."

A sign on the front of a nightclub: FOR MEMBERS AND NONMEMBERS ONLY.

An Army intelligence bulletin during the Vietnam War: "The unit had an estimated strength of 2,000 men, of whom 300 were women."

In response to about a million phone calls, more or less, the name of the book plugged here last week is *The 776 Stupidest Things Ever Said.* Published by Doubleday, $8.99. For that price you get quotes like these:

Marion Barry, when he was mayor of Washington, D.C.: "Aside from all the murders, Washington has one of the lowest crime rates in the country."

Yogi Berra: "If you come to a fork in the road, take it."

A candidate for Congress in Texas: "That low-down scoundrel deserves to be kicked by a jackass, and I'm just the one to do it."

Gerald Ford: "Things are more like they are now than they've ever been."

And a conversation between John Sununu, then governor of New Hampshire, and James A. Baker, Secretary of the Treasury. Sununu: "You're telling us things are so bad because they are so good and they will get better as soon as they get worse?" Baker: "Yes."

Our poll on the question, "Would you rather be president for four years or spend a week in jail?"

Why ask a question like that? Because our polling shows that a great many people now believe the country's problems are so severe that no president can solve them.

People also know that all modern presidents are under intense pressure all time—from their political opponents, from the special interest and letterhead groups, the news media and all those who offer wonderful ideas but want somebody else to pay for them.

So, our poll question again, "Would you rather be president for four years or spend a week in jail?"

The majority—52 percent—said they'd rather go to jail.

A word about one of the annoyances of modern life that could be eliminated if the federal courts would stay out of it.

Your phone rings at home. You answer and get the recorded voice of a telemarketer trying to sell you something. It's no good to say you don't want it because there's no one there to listen. It's only a machine. Even if you hang up, some of these characters will keep your phone line tied up until the sales pitch is finished. Are people supposed to get out of the bathtub to answer calls like that? It's so infuriating Congress passed a law against it.

Now a federal judge has ruled the law unconstitutional, a violation of free speech. The silliest ruling of the year so far. People have the right to free speech, yes. But where does the Constitution give this right to a machine? Has some politician appointed his golf partner to the federal bench? Sounds like it. If the judge has to get out of the tub dripping wet and hear a recorded pitch for lawn chemicals, fine.

Former president George Bush made a speech last night to a business group and will be paid a fee of $100,000—much more than the fees paid to other former presidents for one speech, Reagan or any of them. But there's a little catch now, a new one.

Since Bush left the White House, his successor has put through a very large tax increase for those with high incomes. A few months ago the federal tax on the Bush speech fee would have been $31,000. Now, under Clinton's new tax law, it will be $46,000.

First, he drove Bush out of the White House. Now, when he makes a speech he takes almost half his fee. Doesn't the Constitution forbid cruel and unusual punishment? Is this cruel and unusual? Yes, it is.

All those copper pennies everyone has in a pocket or purse, or piled up in a desk drawer— are they really worth keeping? A new ABC News poll asks the American people the question, should the government continue minting the penny or should we get rid of it? One-third said yes, let them go, they're worth so little now they're hardly worth carrying around.

But there is the problem of the sales tax. Because of it, nothing costs an even amount anymore. It's always 50 cents or $3.00 or whatever, plus tax, always requiring pennies. Could the sales tax exist without cheap calculators? Can anyone figure the 7 1/2 percent tax on a purchase of $16.95 without a calculator? And with people waiting in line behind him? Nobody I know.

A deal all of us retail customers would like, but will never get, is this: we'll give up the penny if you'll give up the sales tax.

Some interesting new research on how the American people decide for and against public and political issues. And they don't decide much of anything based on what the politicians say. They tend not to believe them anymore. They decide based on what they hear from their friends and neighbors at their places of worship, schools, libraries, shopping malls and the check-out lines at supermarkets—places where they talk informally to each other, exchange thoughts and talk about them.

A nonprofit group called the Kettering Foundation had the research done, and David Matthews, former secretary of health, education and welfare published the results. The results are that the American people do not make decisions by listening to politicians, assorted experts and the smart alecks on the editorial pages, radio and television. They listen to their friends, look at their own experience and then decide.

Maybe the best news we've had lately.

They say the Clinton health care plan will be made public in detail this coming week. Of course, we've heard this before, but this time they may actually mean it. Next Wednesday, they say. But maybe Thursday or Friday. They will give us the health care bill, written in government jargon, and it will be 1,600 pages long.

But that's not all. There will also be another separate, additional 800 pages to explain what the 1,600 pages mean. Isn't that decent of them? Shouldn't we be grateful to our government for a favor like that?

November 7, 1993

It may be, as many believe, that the U.S. government does not work very well, takes too much money from us and seldom delivers anything worth what we are forced to pay for it. Social Security may be the only exception. It does pay, and beyond that it may be the most imaginative agency of the government and does try to solve its problems, including this one:

The agency gets 80 million telephone calls a year—people asking various questions. Eighty million. People complain they can't get through. The lines are busy or they're put on hold.

So they talk now of putting the criminals locked up in federal prisons to work answering the phones. When the convicts work, the government pays them 40 cents up to about a dollar an hour. It's cheap help and they can't mug you on the telephone.

Where else can you find a government phone that is answered and have a nice chat with an ax murderer?

A few words about the finely tuned language of the Washington cover-up, language that seemingly admits to something, but on close examination is found to admit nothing. We heard it in the days of Watergate, we heard it when the Marines were blown up in Lebanon, we heard it in discussions of the excessively prolonged Vietnam War, and now we begin to hear it again.

This time we hear it from Hillary Clinton, of all people, in her conversations with *Newsweek* and *Time.* What she said in answer to a question was: "Mistakes were made." Well, we knew that. But it doesn't say what the mistakes were or who made them. But in Washington, that is a skill much admired in the political world—the ability to answer a question without answering it.

It's back again.

Two little scraps of news, one of them a little late.

On this date, April 17, 1492, 502 years ago, Christopher Columbus signed a deal with King Ferdinand and Queen Isabella of Spain to sail westward and see what he could find. Our prediction is that this story will develop into something.

The other is this: I see in the paper one more example of bureaucratic excess, in Hawaii. There a new law says that a barber cannot cut hair until he's had 1,500 hours of training. So it's harder to become a barber than it is to become a member of Congress.

But on the other hand, nobody but a fool would let a member of Congress cut his hair.

A television viewer has recorded and saved a very small news item from a program I did twenty-four years ago, on March 9, 1970, and sent it to me. It's not news anymore, if it ever was, but it's still funny. Here it is, word for word:

In Santa Ana, California, the police found a man living in a trailer and living in there with him were three bears, a donkey, a wallaby, an ocelot, a bobcat, three goats, two opossums, one monkey, three peacocks, thirteen dogs, four cats, six pigeons, five doves, three rabbits, five guinea pigs, one duck, nine chickens, two geese, sixteen quail, two turtles and his wife.

The police removed all of the animals and left him there with his wife.

A few perhaps interesting facts about the new player on the world stage, Kim Jong II, who has inherited the power and the nuclear weapons, if any, in North Korea. So far, since his father died and he took over, we have no report that he's said a word. Not one word. But his country's propaganda machine has done it for him. He's officially been proclaimed a god.

But if he's a god, what does that make his stepmother? She has asserted herself as a figure to be dealt with. When Jimmy Carter visited Pyongyang and they were posing for the official group picture, she elbowed Kim Jong II entirely out of the picture. He's not even in it. So who has the power?

And if he's a god, his tastes are down-to-earth. His great interests are (1) young women, (2) movies and (3) whiskey. Is that godlike?

This week the U.S. Post Office confessed that Washington, D.C., has the slowest mail delivery in the United States. So slow that your bills become overdue even before you get them.

Now we learn that in Washington about 3,900,000 pieces of mail were not delivered but piled up in trailers where they would not be counted as delayed. And included in this mess were huge piles of mail addressed to the federal government.

It is interesting to speculate about what's in that pile of undelivered mail. Maybe a letter from the president asking Congress to carry out his campaign promise to cut taxes for the middle class? That certainly got lost somewhere. Maybe it's in that trailer.

We've all heard about the scandals in the post office—4 million letters piled up in trailers and left there, undelivered. The publicity has led to numerous studies of the problem and how to fix it. So here's how to get your mail delivered on time:

In the post office, the addresses are read by machines. But they can only read printed words. Too dumb to read handwriting.

In Atlanta, for example, there are 128 streets with some form of the word Peachtree in their name.

Mail is delivered faster in the West than in the East.

So here's how to have your mail delivered quickly. Move to Montana. Print the address on a typewriter. And if you live on one of the 128 streets named Peachtree, move.

The big news from Napa, California. They're to have a rodeo. They weren't selling enough tickets, so somebody had the bright idea of promoting the rodeo by driving a herd of cattle through the middle of town. They trucked in twenty-five longhorns and turned them loose and knew right away they'd made a mistake. The first thing the animals did was to start eating the grass and shrubbery in front of the city hall. Then they smashed into the side of the sheriff's car. Then for some reason the herd began trying to push their way into the front door of the Redwood Bank, while three bank employees struggled to hold it shut.

Why would longhorn cattle want to go into the bank? It is a question only a cow could answer.

The day's news from the increasingly famous Denver airport, still unable to open after more than a year. Everyone in the world knows by now that it has problems with its baggage-handling machinery. State-of-the-art, they said, when they put it in. But it turned out that bags checked to one city would have been sent to another. If it went anywhere at all. In the course of the tests, some of it was chewed to bits by the machinery. Passengers' belongings strewn around the baggage room—shirts, socks and shaving cream scattered around in a mess.

So for more than a year the new billion-dollar airport has not been able to open. But the highway signs pointing to the airport entrance are still there and I have heard complaints from several people that they followed the signs, wound up at a nonworking airport and missed their flights.

Now comes the news that the runways, never even used, are cracking and sinking into holes in the ground. In this high-tech age, what will they do? Fill the holes with chewed-up baggage?

W hat are we to make of this?

Cuba is in turmoil, people are hungry, and Fidel Castro blames us.

Haiti is in turmoil, people are hungry, and the military leaders blame us.

Iraq is in turmoil and Saddam Hussein blames us.

If a country is to be judged by its enemies, Americans should be rather proud. Maybe it is best for a country to be loved, but next best is to be hated by the right people. We are.

A brief look at the checkered history of Haiti's Duvalier family, beginning with the first president-for-life, François, known as Papa Doc. He was a doctor of some kind, but it is not certain that he cured more people than he killed. His hobby was torturing his enemies and listening to their screams. I have seen his lavish torture chamber in the basement of his presidential palace.

Once I was doing a documentary about Haiti and asked him for an interview. He said yes, but only if he could write out my questions and write out his answers.

He died and passed the office on to his son, Jean-Claude, called Baby Doc, who perhaps was not ready for political leadership. At the age of twenty-one, he was still playing with dolls. The Haitians say that when he was driven out he stole $125 million and took the money with him to Paris, where he remains.

But, sad to report, he's broke now. Wine, women, high rents, child support and all that. Paris is an expensive city.

A sort of sweet-sad little tale. Stanley New-berg, an Austrian, fled the persecution of the Jews and came to this country. He worked with his father, a fruit peddler on the Lower East Side of New York City. Years passed, he got into the aluminum business, did well and wound up own-ing the company he worked in for years.

He died. He was eighty-one. He left $5,600,000. Left it to the U.S. government. He said in his will: "It is my expression of deep grat-itude for living in this kind of government, notwithstanding its inequities." The Bureau of Public Debt took his 5 million 6.

The sad part is that the government spends $4.1 billion a day. So Mr. Newberg's $5 million, generously given, will disappear in less than two minutes.

From the annals of bureaucracy. Consider the town of Moffett, Oklahoma, population 340. Nothing whatever has happened there since last year when a chicken factory tried to dump its sludge on the edge of town and there was a fight over who would haul it away.

Now this has happened: under the new crime bill passed by Congress, cities and towns get money to fight crime by expanding their police departments. Moffett, Oklahoma, was handed $106,000 to expand its police department, but it doesn't have one.

They did have one officer named Jimmy Jones who rode up and down the four blocks of Main Street in a seven-year-old Pontiac fighting crime when he could find any. He found so little they fired him. Now the town has no police department. So who gets the $106,000?

I think they should give it to the mayor of Moffett, David Carolina by name, who has to earn extra money by collecting aluminum beer cans and turning them in for the deposits. Surely he needs the money more than anyone else.

In the race for a Senate seat from California, it appears that the two candidates—Dianne Feinstein and Michael Huffington—will set a new world record for campaign spending. Before it's all over, $40 million, maybe? Or more?

So to run in a big state you have to be rich or have rich and generous friends. Michael Huffington doesn't need generous friends. He has his family's oil money and he's been spending it hand over fist. He's spending more than $20 million to win a job that in six years—if he wins—will yield less than one-twentieth of what the job cost him.

Is anyone who will make a financial deal like that qualified to handle the public's money?

It's interesting to see that this week the American people voted to do a lot of legislating on their own, leaving the politicians out of it.

For example: Oregon and Colorado voted to define obscenity, even though a Supreme Court justice once said he couldn't define it but he knew it when he saw it.

In ten states they voted on all kinds of gambling casinos, lotteries, slot machines at the airport, blackjack and poker tables on riverboats. The states see easy money. Maybe.

A county in Oregon voted on giving each homeowner a gun.

Another Oregon vote would stop the use of dogs to hunt bear.

Alaska, for the fourth time, voted on moving the state capital from Juneau to another town, the present capital being totally inaccessible by land.

In Oklahoma there was a vote on allowing wine makers to use grapes from out of state.

And in Washington State there was a vote on

allowing people to buy false teeth directly from the makers and without seeing a dentist.

Democratic self-government covers all things great and small.

We do get news—or something—from around the world. How about this from a newspaper clipping somebody sent to me from a courtroom trial in Accra, Ghana, in Africa? A police officer told the judge he had stopped a Ford Escort for speeding. He testified he'd looked inside the car and thought the family in the car, as he put it, "were all very ugly." On closer inspection, he told the judge, he found that the passengers in the Ford were all goats, all of them pregnant, and all of them wearing T-shirts.

Don't ask. I don't know.

The big national electronics convention is now on in Las Vegas, Nevada. This is where the industry displays its new models of all kinds of electronic gadgets and gear. The big new thing in television now is projection sets. Because people want bigger pictures. And the familiar TV set with the picture on the front of a box has grown to be about as big as it can get. Make it any larger, they say, and you couldn't get it through the door of a house. That would make it hard to sell, wouldn't it?

What else is new is this: computers now outsell television sets. This is true even though it is said that 70 percent of the American people do not know how to use computers. What do they do with them? I haven't any idea.

A little real estate news—houses for sale, unfurnished. The prices negotiable. But the commuting time may be inconvenient. They're all castles in East Germany.

They once belonged to kings, queens, counts and so on—like a full-scale chess set. The German government wants to sell them to anyone who will preserve them. Fairy tales for sale, they call it.

A story I heard in London: a young couple rented one of these German castles for a summer. Fields of grapes and a winery came along with it. They made some wine, invited friends from London to visit. One afternoon they sat in one of the turrets and served the wine, saying to their guests: "This wine came from grapes right here, six feet away." They tasted the wine and said, "It doesn't travel well, does it?"

The day after tomorrow is Valentine's Day, our annual celebration of love, usually expressed with cute little cards from Hallmark, flowers or Whitman's Samplers.

But an altogether different kind of Valentine appeared in Jackson, Georgia. A woman named Mary Popp wanted to express her affection for a man named Carl Isaacs; the inconvenient fact was that Isaacs was in jail, charged with murder.

But, as they say, love will find a way. So Mary Popp sent Isaacs a box of cookies with a 12-inch hacksaw inside. The police found it, and now they're both in jail. In separate cells.

In these early months of the year, many state legislatures are in session. Even so, it's clear the country will survive a lot of idiotic nonsense.

For example, in Oregon there's a bill saying anyone who keeps a vicious dog will be punished by having his welfare cut. What if he's not on welfare? It doesn't say.

In the Montana legislature, they're angry because the government wants to bring wolves back into the West, threatening their cattle. So they've demanded that wolves be brought into other places, including Central Park in the middle of New York City.

In Wisconsin a hunter landing his small airplane on a grass strip hit a deer and killed him, only to find he couldn't keep it because this was considered hunting without a license. Now a bill in the legislature says if you kill a deer with an airplane, you can keep it.

A little news that is either financial or literary. It's not clear which. Speaker Newt Gingrich, on *Larry King Live* Friday night, said his $4.5 million deal with a book publisher was a mistake, he shouldn't have done it, it was naïve. And all the complaints from members of Congress took attention away from the Republican legislative program, he said.

But one point was never mentioned, even by those who say they're worried about the federal deficit and debt. If Gingrich had taken the $4.5 million, the government would have made out very well. Because about half the money—around two and a quarter million—would have gone for taxes.

Half for Newt and half for taxes. Which half were they complaining about?

Washington in the years before World War II. The White House had no fence, front or back. It was just another public building.

A local resident was driving down Pennsylvania Avenue in his Ford convertible when it began to rain. He pulled in under the White House portico out of the rain and got out to put up his canvas top. A presidential usher came out and gave him a hand. He said thanks and drove away.

On clear days, young employees of the government brought sandwiches in brown paper sacks and ate them sitting around on the White House lawn. That's how it was.

Until, during World War II, they built an iron fence. Then came floodlights, alarms, armed guards.

Today, given the terrorism in what once was a peaceful country, the stretch of Pennsylvania Avenue in front of the White House has been closed off altogether for security reasons. Now you can't even drive by and look at it.

A sad day. Another one.

A man in Utah called the police and said his wife of three and a half years was missing. The police searched and found his wife and also found his wife was not a woman but a man.

The husband said he never knew it. People will wonder why not. The obvious questions I will leave to your imagination. But I do wonder why he was not suspicious when he watched his wife lather up her face and shave. The Washington *Post* asked why he didn't wonder when she asked for a Christmas gift of a drill press.

The husband now wants an annulment on grounds of irreconcilable differences. Very likely the court will agree.

Asked about all this, the husband said, "I feel pretty stupid."

August 13, 1995

I have no idea what to say about this, so I will briefly give the facts. In the Oklahoma state prison a man sentenced to death for murder was to be executed in a few hours. He said while he waited he would like to take a nap. That alone was bizarre enough—sleeping through his last hours of life. But when the prison guards came to wake him up, he was out, unconscious. He had taken an overdose of something, apparently in a suicide attempt. They rushed him to a hospital, had him revived, then brought him back to the prison, where they executed him.

This is not ninettenth-century Italian opera. It is twentieth-century truth.

David Brinkley was born in Wilmington, North Carolina, and was educated at the University of North Carolina and Vanderbilt University. His career as a disseminator and interpreter of the news began early—while still in high school he wrote for his hometown paper, the Wilmington *Morning Star.* After his army service in World War II he worked for United Press and then joined NBC News, becoming White House correspondent before the end of the war. In 1956 he and Chet Huntley launched their celebrated news program *The Huntley-Brinkley Report,* which during its fourteen years won them every major broadcasting award. He then became coanchor (with John Chancellor), and subsequently commentator, on *NBC Nightly News,* and since 1981 has conducted his own ABC program of news commentary and interviews, *This Week with David Brinkley,* on Sunday mornings. He has been the recipient of ten Emmy Awards and three George Foster Peabody Awards. He lives with his wife, Susan, in Washington, D.C.

Look for these at your local bookstore

American Heart Association, *American Heart Association
    Cookbook, 5th Edition Abridged*
Ben Artzi-Pelossof, Noa, *In the Name of Sorrow and Hope*
Benchley, Peter, *White Shark*
Berendt, John, *Midnight in the Garden of Good and Evil*
Bradford, Barbara Taylor, *Angel*
Brando, Marlon with Robert Lindsey, *Brando:
    Songs My Mother Taught Me*
Brinkley, David, *David Brinkley*
Buscaglia, Leo, Ph.D., *Born for Love*
Byatt, A. S., *Babel Tower*
Ciaro, Joe, editor, *The Random House Large Print Book
    of Jokes and Anecdotes*
Crichton, Michael, *Disclosure*
Crichton, Michael, *The Lost World*
Cruz Smith, Martin, *Rose*
Daley, Rosie, *In the Kitchen with Rosie*
Doctorow, E. L., *The Waterworks*
Dunne, Dominick, *A Season in Purgatory*
Flagg, Fannie, *Daisy Fay and the Miracle Man*
Flagg, Fannie, *Fried Green Tomatoes at the
    Whistle Stop Cafe*
Follett, Ken, *A Place Called Freedom*
Fulghum, Robert, *From Beginning to End: The Rituals of
    Our Lives*
Fulghum, Robert, *It Was on Fire When I Lay Down
    on It*
Fulghum, Robert, *Maybe (Maybe Not): Second Thoughts
    from a Secret Life*
García Márquez, Gabriel, *Of Love and Other Demons*

(continued)

Gilman, Dorothy, *Mrs. Pollifax and the Lion Killer*
Grimes, Martha, *The Horse You Came In On*
Grimes, Martha, *Rainbow's End*
Grimes, Martha, *Hotel Paradise*
Halberstam, David, *The Fifties* (2 volumes)
Hepburn, Katharine, *Me*
James, P. D., *The Children of Men*
James, P. D., *Original Sin*
Koontz, Dean, *Dark Rivers of the Heart*
Koontz, Dean, *Icebound*
Koontz, Dean, *Intensity*
Krantz, Judith, *Dazzle*
Krantz, Judith, *Lovers*
Krantz, Judith, *Scruples Two*
Krantz, Judith, *Spring Collection*
Landers, Ann, *Wake Up and Smell the Coffee!*
le Carré, John, *Our Game*
Lindbergh, Anne Morrow, *Gift from the Sea*
Ludlum, Robert, *The Road to Omaha*
Mayle, Peter, *Anything Considered*
McCarthy, Cormac, *The Crossing*
Meadows, Audrey with Joe Daley, *Love, Alice*
Michener, James A., *Mexico*
Michener, James A., *Miracle in Seville*
Michener, James A., *Recessional*
Mother Teresa, *A Simple Path*
Nuland, Sherwin B., *How We Die*
Patterson, Richard North, *Eyes of a Child*
Patterson, Richard North, *The Final Judgment*
Pavarotti, Luciano and William Wright, *Pavarotti: My World*
Phillips, Louis, editor, *The Random House Large Print Treasury of Best-Loved Poems*
Pope John Paul II, *Crossing the Threshold of Hope*
Pope John Paul II, *The Gospel of Life*

(continued)

Powell, Colin with Joseph E. Persico, *My American Journey*
Rendell, Ruth, *Simisola*
Riva, Maria, *Marlene Dietrich* (2 volumes)
Rooney, Andy, *My War*
Shaara, Jeff, *Gods and Generals*
Truman, Margaret, *Murder at the National Gallery*
Tyler, Anne, *Ladder of Years*
Tyler, Anne, *Saint Maybe*
Updike, John, *Rabbit at Rest*